Getting a Ph.D. in Economics

Stuart J. Hillmon

PENN

UNIVERSITY OF PENNSYLVANIA PRESS

PHILADELPHIA

Published by
University of Pennsylvania Press
Philadelphia, Pennsylvania 19104-4112
www.upenn.edu/pennpress

Printed in the United States of America on acid-free paper
10 9 8 7 6 5 4 3 2 1

Library of Congress Cataloging-in-Publication Data
Hillmon, Stuart J.
     Getting a Ph.D. in economics / Stuart J. Hillmon. — 1st ed.
        p. cm.
     Includes bibliographical references and index.
     ISBN 978-0-8122-2288-3 (hardcover : alk. paper)
        1. Economics—Study and teaching (Graduate)—United States.
2. Economics—Vocational guidance—United States. 3. Graduate students—
Vocational guidance—United States. I. Title.
HB74.8.H56 2014
330.071'173—dc23
                                                                                   2013031743

Contents

Chapter 1

Preliminaries: The Lowdown on Academic Economics and Ph.D. Programs

So you're thinking of going to graduate school in economics. I applaud your good taste and discernment. Now is the right time to study economics. Thanks to *Freakonomics* and blog- and op-ed-wielding economists, we Ph.D. economists seem almost cool; not only can we analyze the stock market, we know something about sumo wrestling. And more of us economists are wanted and needed. The financial crisis of 2008 and the Great Recession have made it abundantly clear how important it is to have people around who know and understand what's going on in the economy.

But there are many misconceptions about economics and about graduate economics training. The purpose of this book is to introduce you to the world of academic economics by way of a guide through a Ph.D. program in economics. My goal is to have you come out with a clear-eyed view of what is required to become an academic (research) economist, and to equip you with the required tools.

But before we get started on your graduate school adventure, we need to take a step back: we need to double-check your sanity. By this I mean we need to make sure you are clear on the (real) purpose of a Ph.D. program in economics and on what exactly it is that this program is meant to do. Graduate school is not all rainbows and unicorns, but it has a chance of coming pretty close if you understand why you're there.

The (Real) Purpose of a Ph.D. Program in Economics

To start with the obvious, Ph.D. programs are unlike any other graduate program. In particular, a distinction is always made between Ph.D. programs and "professional" graduate programs like law school, medical school, or business school. These professional programs are intended to train you in a profession—namely, law, medicine, and business. Ph.D. programs, in contrast, are all about the life of the mind and scholarship and thinking heavy thoughts, and indeed, a good Ph.D. program includes all of these things.

But Ph.D. programs, even if they aren't so-named, *are* also professional programs. You should never forget that the purpose of a Ph.D. program in economics is to train you in the *profession* of economic research. Put differently, a Ph.D. program in economics is meant to train you to become a research professor in economics. It is not meant to train you to be a quant jock on Wall Street or a policy maker in Washington.

That's right, the purpose of Ph.D. programs in economics is to produce research professors in economics; there is no other purpose. Of course, many students who graduate with Ph.D.s in economics go on to do other interesting and important things like working on Wall Street or making public policy, but few programs and even fewer faculty would say that these other things are what economics programs are designed to train students to do.

Many students who enter Ph.D. programs are largely unaware of this primary purpose. Yet, if you come into these programs without having adopted this very purpose for yourself, you may well be surprised if not downright miserable.

Here's an example that is more concrete. Suppose you decided to go to law school, not because you wanted to be a lawyer, but because you thought that law school might be useful for, say, starting your own car repair shop. Repair shop owners occasionally get sued, so it would be useful for a car repair shop owner to know something about law. What would your experience of law school be like? You would be unhappy with professors who were teaching you constitutional law and criminal procedure, which have nothing to do with your interests. You would be unhappy with fellow students who talked about case *this* and precedent *that* all the time. You would be crying over the boring cases you were forced to study. By and large, you would be miserable and would find the curriculum, faculty, and students intolerably narrow. While you might find a course or two useful for the car repair business, law school is primarily meant to train lawyers, not entrepreneurial auto mechanics.

Likewise, if you go into a Ph.D. program in economics to do something other than to become a research professor in economics, you will be deeply unhappy. If you are, however, clear from the start about what the real purpose of this program is, there is some chance that you will benefit a great deal from the program and even enjoy it.

What Academic Economists Do

Let's make a distinction between what Ph.D. economists do and what academic or research Ph.D. economists—i.e. economists with Ph.D.s sitting in universities or research institutes—do. You may see economists with Ph.D. degrees doing lots of interesting things. They advise presidents; they consult for firms, banks, and investment companies; they study economic trends; they analyze public policy and make policy recommendations; they teach undergraduate and graduate students.

Academic economists do fewer interesting things. They can act as advisors and consultants, but that is not their primary job. They may be expected to teach and advise students but in many places that is not their main job either. The main job of an academic economist is to write research articles and publish them.

Writing and publishing articles is not easy. It requires understanding the existing academic economics literature, contributing in original ways to it, and convincing other academic economists that you've just done something interesting. This summary is a highly abbreviated version of academic economics but it is pretty accurate.

A crucial missing piece of information, though, is this mysterious thing called "the academic economics literature" that economists are supposed to know and contribute to. These days, this literature is highly mathematical and can be very abstract. Much of the literature has relevance to the real world, but the applications may not be obvious to those unfamiliar with the current jargon and methods of academic economics. This is where the Ph.D. program comes in. The first two years of a Ph.D. program in economics are designed to teach you what the profession considers to be the most important aspects of the current economics literature. The rest of the program is designed to train you to be able to contribute to this literature.

Bad and Good Reasons for Doing a Ph.D. in Economics

There are perhaps two good reasons to study for a Ph.D. in economics and about 3,007 bad reasons. Here are the top four bad yet unnervingly common reasons that students enter Ph.D. programs in economics:

1. You're generally smart and did well in school but you don't know what to do next with your life.
2. You can't find a job, and it's a good holding pattern until you can get one (plus, you can get a master's degree in economics, which is as good as an M.B.A.).
3. You want to make lots of money.
4. You want to work in public policy and save the world.

Let's unpack each of these and see why they won't work so well.

**1. You're generally smart and did well in school but you don't know
what to do next with your life.**

While professors in the academy are all for having smart graduate
students who did well in school, Ph.D. programs are a terrible place
to be if you aren't quite sure what to do next. The main reason for
this is because Ph.D. programs are narrower in their focus than almost any other graduate program that you might consider. You will
surely get an immersion baptism in graduate economics, but this
turns out to be much, much narrower than you might think based
on your undergraduate economics classes.

If you are unsure of what you want to do next, a brutal first year
(and all economics programs are brutal in their first year) in a specialized field will surely not help you explore or find things you want
to do. In fact, a bad first year can jeopardize your chances of ever
doing economics again, should you want to pick it up later, because
fewer programs will take a chance on you. So if you don't know what
to do, going to a Ph.D. program in economics will definitely not help
you know where to go and it might even close off future prospects.

**2. You can't find a job, and it's a good holding pattern until you can get
one (plus, you can get a master's degree in economics, which is as good
as an M.B.A.).**

Unless you have very screwy preferences, it is not clear that being
forced to study a difficult, technical, narrow subject is better than
being unemployed. You will get paid beans during grad school (if
you're lucky), and you will certainly not have time to sleep, much
less go job-hunting, while you're in grad school.

And we should dispense here and now with this fallacy that a
master's degree in economics is as good as an M.B.A. While there is
practical utility to be gained from M.B.A. coursework, much of the
benefit of an M.B.A. program is in getting to know your classmates—
working professionals who may be helpful in your business career—
and in the career services offered to M.B.A. students. So, if you get

a master's in economics, not only will you be forced to take courses that are much more technically demanding, time consuming, and less relevant for the business world, you will also extract none of the most important benefits of an M.B.A. program. And the average business employer is much more interested in hiring an M.B.A. graduate—a quantity she knows—than a master's in economics graduate.

3. You want to make lots of money.

Snort. Not sure this deserves comment. Obviously, if you want to make lots of money, you should get an M.B.A. instead of a Ph.D. in economics; this fact has been empirically confirmed many times over.

4. You want to work in public policy and save the world.

While this is more feasible than reason number 3, getting a Ph.D. in economics is an awful lot of work to prepare for a job in public policy. Much policy work that has any real-world relevance requires very little of the abstruse mathematical juggling that is the bread and butter of economics programs. Further, economics programs won't teach you anything about saving the world, and you probably won't save the world either. Although many economists do act as policy advisors, getting a Ph.D. in economics is a more difficult path than alternative paths that can also lead to working in policy and saving the world.[1]

Those are four bad reasons for wanting to do a Ph.D. in economics. Now here are two good reasons:

1. You want to do economic research, you have questions you're interested in answering, and you have ideas about how to answer them.
2. You want to teach economics at the university level.

Some people might even argue that reason number 1 is the *only* good reason for doing a Ph.D. in economics. I include teaching as reason number 2 because: (1) it is an empirical reality that many colleges and universities will only hire Ph.D. graduates for their teaching positions; and (2) almost all academic economics positions require you to both teach and do research, even if the pay and promotion incentives are based on your research. To the extent that you think you might enjoy teaching economics at the university level as well as conducting economic research, these are the two best reasons to get a Ph.D. in economics.[2]

Going to Grad School Now

Suppose this all sounds good to you, but you're not quite sure if now is the right time. Perhaps you did blindingly well in college, but you're feeling a little burnt out and need a break. Or you are tired of being poor and you would like to spend a couple of years making some serious money. In general, if you have other things that you want to do with your life right now (make money, travel the world, play in a band), you should go and do them. Grad school will still be here.

Once you start on the econ grad school track, it will be all-consuming and you should be intellectually and personally prepared for the challenge. It's not easy to take a break during grad school and get back on track. If you're not 100 percent sure that you're ready right now, the time away from school will scratch that (non-economic) itch and might make you even more keen to come back. Indeed, many students who jump into grad school without giving much thought to other things they might want to do regret not having pursued these other options before grad school.

Now, you may be concerned that if you don't go to grad school right now, your skills will deteriorate. It is true if you spend time away from doing economics and math, you will be a little creaky when you come back. As long as your time away is not more than two or three years, though, it will not take too long for you to recall the things you learned and get up to speed, so this should not be a particular worry. The most important thing is that you have taken the time to fulfill any other ambitions you might have. Grad school is like marriage, a long-term relationship requiring a serious commitment; it's probably a good idea to date around a little before you get married.

Economics Versus Friends of Economics

Students often wonder if they really want to be in a Ph.D. program in economics, as opposed to a program in a closely related field. These days, you can get a Ph.D. in public policy, finance, business economics, political economy, or health economics. Why not one of those?

A Ph.D. program in economics is not the right choice for everyone, but before deciding whether to devote yourself to economics or to a field friendly to economics (hereafter referred to as FOE, friend of economics), you should know that economics and FOE degrees are not easily substitutable. There are obvious differences in curriculum, and related to that and perhaps more important, there are differences in job opportunities. While economics Ph.D. graduates can and do find employment in economics departments, business schools, political science departments, and health policy departments in medical schools, Ph.D. graduates of these FOE programs are typically employable only in FOE departments *even if they are working on exactly the same topic that an economics graduate is.* Unfair but true. What's more, in certain FOE departments, economics graduates may still have an advantage over FOE graduates; that is, an economics graduate may have a better chance of being employed at some public policy schools than a public policy graduate.[3] Thus, economics graduates generally have a wider range of employment opportunities than FOE graduates.

If you are unsure of your area of interest within economics or if you are keen to have the broader training afforded by economics, an econ program would be a better option for you. If you are very sure of your research interests and don't want to waste your time taking courses not related to them, a FOE program is a better choice. In some programs, the courses and qualifying exams you take are identical to those required of economics students, but you take fewer of them. For example, business economics students may be required to take the same microeconomics and econometrics courses as the economics students, but are excused from macroeconomics courses. You should also know that, not only do FOE programs have a narrower focus, they also tend to have a more applied focus, and this is reflected in the content of the courses and in faculty research interests.

Having noted the differences between the two types of programs, I should of course mention that despite these differences, the advice in this book is helpful for Ph.D. FOE students as well as econ students. Notwithstanding the curricular and labor market differences, the structure of FOE programs is very similar to that of economics programs, and FOE students and economics students face many of the same academic and professional issues.

Master's Degrees

If you are interested in a Ph.D. program in economics, should you get a master's degree first? Perhaps you're unsure of whether you really would like to commit to a Ph.D. program and just want to dip your toes in the water. Or your undergraduate degree was not in economics and you're thinking about doing a Ph.D. in economics.

In the United States, the master's degree is usually conferred as doctoral students progress through the program; there are few terminal master's programs in economics. This is changing somewhat as more mid-level departments are offering the master's degree option; in addition, a few respected economics departments have in recent years begun offering terminal master's degrees (for example, Boston University, Duke, and New York University). There are also good master's degree programs overseas. Many top universities in Europe (e.g., Cambridge, London School of Economics, Oxford, and Universitat Pompeu Fabra in Spain) offer terminal master's programs and confer degrees that are well-respected in the United States.

Bear in mind that these programs will be demanding and technical. They consist of the first year of coursework in a Ph.D. program and cover perhaps the least fun part of any graduate program.

If you want to dip your toes in the graduate economics water, a master's program is not a bad idea.[4] It will help you get your skill set together, help you find out if you enjoy graduate study in economics, and show others that you are serious about economics. If you do go on for your Ph.D., your experience during the first year of your Ph.D. will be much more pleasant because you will have seen a lot of the same material in your master's program.

There are some downsides, however. In many master's programs, and especially the overseas master's programs, there is very little funding so you will have to fund yourself. Second, in many European programs, exams take place only once a year. American students have difficulty knowing how to study for these kinds of exams and good students can do poorly on them; a whole year's worth of work and tuition, and your Ph.D. admission prospects, may go down the tubes if you have a bad day or two so it's a bit of a risk.

By the way, you should also know that a master's degree in economics has little professional value beyond getting you into a better Ph.D. economics program than you would have otherwise gotten into (although of course it has intellectual value). As I mentioned above, it is a poor substitute for an M.B.A. or, say, a master's in public policy. So if you decide to go for your master's degree, do it with the understanding that its only value will be to help you prepare for your Ph.D.

A Few Factoids About Economics Ph.D. Programs

So much for the highly opinionated part of this chapter. Now for a few facts. You may be curious to know some general statistics about economics Ph.D. programs.

I should note that, here and throughout the book, I will focus primarily on economics training in the United States. Although the economics profession has become much more globalized in recent decades and there are many excellent economists and doctoral economics programs overseas, most advanced economics training still occurs in U.S. programs. (There is also more heterogeneity in the structure of non-U.S. training programs compared to U.S. programs.) My U.S. focus should be interpreted simply as reflecting the system I know best and as an attempt at addressing the needs of the majority of economics students, rather than as a dismissal of non-U.S. alternatives.

According to the American Economic Association (AEA), there are 136 Ph.D. programs in economics in the United States. There are no official estimates of the total number of students in these programs, but several back-of-the-envelope calculations suggest the number is around 10,000.[5] The top fifteen programs tend to have more students than the lower-ranked programs; an estimate from the 1980s suggests that program enrollment in the top fifteen programs averages around 130 students, whereas enrollment in lower-ranked programs averages around 50–70 students (Hansen 1991).

Since the 1970s, there have been steady increases in the percentage of doctorates in economics awarded to women. In 1977, about 9 percent of economics doctorates were awarded to women; in 1987, this proportion was 19 percent; and in 2001, it was 28 percent (Siegfried and Stock 2004).

There have also been increases in the percentage of economics doctorates awarded to non-U.S. citizens. In 1977, about 33 percent of economics doctorates were awarded to non-U.S. citizens; by 2001, this percentage had increased to 62 percent (Siegfried and Stock 2004).

And finally one last statistic: how long will take you to finish? Had you had the foresight and fetal know-how to graduate in 1977, the median time to completion would have been 5.7 years. Time to completion has been steadily increasing, and in 2001, the median time to Ph.D. was 7 years (Siegfried and Stock 2004).

If these and other fun cocktail-party facts interest you, you can find more in the papers listed in the American Economic Association's extensive bibliography of studies on graduate economics education (URL below). For now, I'm presenting you with a few facts about economics Ph.D. programs because it's always good to know about the institution to which you are committing yourself. But overall statistics can only say so much. Mostly my job is to inform you about the *experience* of being a graduate student.

Still here? Consider yourself briefed on economics Ph.D. programs and their real purpose (to produce professors). If after reading this chapter, you are still keen and are ready to make a serious commitment to such a program, read on.

Notes

1. To be fair, I should also say that among those working in policy, people with Ph.D. degrees (in economics, political science, public policy, or some other domain) will likely have more decision-making authority than policy analysts with master's degrees, so there is that additional value of a Ph.D. in economics within the policy arena.

2. I would not, however, recommend emphasizing your love of teaching in your Ph.D. application.

3. One exception is finance departments, where Ph.D. finance graduates have an advantage over Ph.D. economics graduates.

4. If you did not study economics as an undergraduate, you might want to try a Diploma program in economics before attempting a master's program. These Diploma programs, primarily found in the United Kingdom, cover the curriculum of undergraduate economics and can give you more background on the intuition of economics before you jump into its more technical parts.

5. We can obtain the 10,000 number several different ways. First, we can calculate a rough estimate based on the assumption that there are about thirty students in each program's starting cohort, with an average time to completion of seven years, and an overall 50 percent graduation rate after ten years. Similarly, we can work backward using the same time-to-completion and graduation rates and observe that there are about 1100 Ph.D. economics graduates on the market each year. We can also use data from the 1980s reported by Hansen (1991) and inflate it a bit to account for the expansion of graduate programs over the past thirty years. In Hansen's summary of the findings of the AEA's Commission on Graduate Education in Economics, he states that enrollment in the six Tier 1 programs (identified by the National Research Council as Chicago, Harvard, MIT, Princeton, Stanford, and Yale) and nine

Tier 2 programs (identified as Columbia, Michigan, Minnesota, Northwestern, Pennsylvania, Rochester, UC–Berkeley, UCLA, and UW–Madison) averaged about 130 students; enrollment in the remaining programs was on average 50–70. All three calculations give us similar ballpark estimates of 10,000.

References

Hansen, W. Lee. 1991. "The Education and Training of Economics Doctorates: Major Findings of the Executive Secretary of the American Economic Association's Commission on Graduate Education in Economics." *Journal of Economic Literature* 29: 1054–1087.

Siegfried, John J., and Wendy A. Stock. 2004. "The Market for New Ph.D. Economists in 2002." *American Economics Review Papers and Proceedings* 94: 272–285.

Useful Web Pages

American Economic Association, Research on Economics Graduate Education page: http://www.aeaweb.org/gradstudents/Education_Issues.php.

Chapter 2

Applying to Ph.D. Programs: It's Both What You Know and Who You Know

So you've done the requisite amount of navel gazing and decided that you do indeed want to apply to Ph.D. programs in economics. The process seems straightforward: write a one-page statement about your favorite subject (yourself), ask a few professors for letters of reference, and glue your bottom to a chair for a couple of hours to take the Graduate Record Examinations (GRE). Aside from parting with your hard-earned money for the application fees, the process doesn't seem too painful.

And it isn't painful. It is also not as straightforward as it seems. Sure, the *mechanics* of the process are clear—just as, say, the mechanics of running a marathon are clear: just put one foot ahead of the other, then repeat for the next 26.2 miles. But would you expect to finish the race if you decided to do nothing else but just show up on the day of the marathon?

If you wanted to run a marathon, you would have needed to train for a couple of months, figured out when to drink Gatorade and when to stop at the Porta-Potty, and found out which running gear worked for you so you don't get blisters in unpleasant places. Similarly, to complete a successful application, you need to be prepared. You can't just cough up an essay overnight and lie in your hammock waiting for those acceptances to roll in. You need to have thought hard about what the graduate programs want, and figured out the best way to present yourself to them *before* you sit down to fill out those applications. You don't have to be obsessive or Machiavellian about it, but you do need to be smart and pragmatic.

Inside the Head of the Graduate Admissions Director

Now the last place we want to be is inside the head of the admissions director, but in the interest of pedagogy, let's take a short field trip. The admissions director is likely some tenured professor who has volunteered for this job because he has been promised lots of goodies (e.g., less teaching, a promotion) if he agrees to do so. He may also vaguely care about the kinds of students who are populating his department. Perhaps he thinks the current students are too narrow or too unprepared or not suited to his own research interests; he can now have the fairly expansive and often unchecked power of deciding who gets in the door.

The modern admissions director sometimes has others assisting him. These assistants are other professors who have volunteered to be on the admissions committee, and are delegated to read the files and give them some kind of numerical score. These people also vaguely care about finding the kinds of students with whom they would like to work (or, equivalently, who might be good research assistants for them). There may also be other faculty members who, because they are either hapless or inexplicably conscientious, have volunteered to be screeners; they go through the files at a maniacal pace and do the quick first cut of the files.

The admissions director has to manage his own preferences, the department's stated objectives ("get better macro students!"), other faculty's preferences (especially those of the powerful faculty), and perhaps his relationship with his colleagues in other departments at other universities. At the same time, he has a limited number of departmental fellowships and university fellowships which he had to wrest away from the Dean. He may also be interested in (or be forced to be interested in) issues of ethnic, gender, and other kinds of diversity. So you see, this is one conflicted person.

But enough about *his* mental health. The purpose of this tour was to show you how politically complicated the admissions process can be, and that it is not simply a matter of "merit" and hoping that people will see past your bad grade in linear algebra and clearly see the real you. On the other hand, I do not want to be deeply cynical and tell you that it is about who you know as opposed to what you know; being very good does help, being very prepared helps as well, and really wanting to and being willing to make the commitment to be a Ph.D. economist is important.

The point of this discussion is that the only people who don't have to worry about the admissions process are those with stunningly good undergraduate records from top-ranked universities who have ridiculously glowing letters of recommendation and perfect GRE scores, and have already published a paper in *Econometrica*. Fortunately, there are not enough of these people to populate all of the graduate programs of U.S. economics departments, so the admissions committees have to sift through the rest of us.

Because of the political nuances that I mentioned, there is some idiosyncrasy in the admissions process. There will be a small subset of students who will get in everywhere, but most students are not in this position. While you may hope that politics will work in your favor, you will likely not be privy to the political battles within each department so you cannot consistently leverage the internal politics.

What you can do, however, is to be prepared. Most students are quite careless with their applications, viewing them as a big hassle, and putting them together in a slap-dash way at the last minute. If you come in knowledgeable about what the admissions director wants and show that you have what he wants, you will avoid being swept out with these sloppy amateurs. This will give you a better chance of getting one of those idiosyncratic slots and can ensure your place in one or two of your top-choice departments even if you can't get offers from all of them.

Characteristics of Successful Candidates

Successful applicants to Ph.D. programs are likely to have the following in their portfolio:

1. high quantitative reasoning GRE scores
2. coursework and good grades in technically demanding economics courses (e.g., game theory, mathematical economics), advanced undergraduate math courses (e.g., real analysis, abstract algebra), and formal statistics courses (probability theory, statistical theory)
3. strong letters of recommendation from (prominent) economists whom the other departments know and trust
4. evidence of research experience in the subfield of economics in which they wish to specialize
5. seriousness of intellectual purpose and commitment to academic economics

Let's take each of these in turn.

GRE Scores

First, the GRE scores. There are two facts you should know about the GRE. One, it is typically only ever used as a screening device. That is, from the 500 or however many applications the department gets, it tosses out the 350 applications with the lowest GRE scores right away. That's right: your application, your carefully crafted statement of purpose, none of it gets read if your GRE score does not make the initial cut. Top departments have no qualms about cutting applicants with scores lower than the 99th percentile on the quantitative reasoning section, and even then, they are still left with too many applicants. In general, departments that are lower-ranked or are more diverse in their portfolio of research interests tend to have lower GRE cutoffs. Even so, the quantitative reasoning GRE standard for all economics programs is still very high compared to some other social science programs.

Many economics departments will report the median GRE score or the range of GRE scores of their students or admitted applicants. Information on the median to the top of the range is useful in assessing your chances of being admitted by a certain department. If your GRE score is above the median, then your file has some chance of being read. The lower end of the range is misleading, however. Often, the students with the low-end GRE scores were admitted through some special exception (e.g., they have been a research assistant for a professor in the department, they came highly recommended by another professor).

The second thing you should know is that the only scores economics departments look at are the scores from the quantitative reasoning section. This is so for two reasons. First, you don't need to be a fluent or even passable English speaker to be a good economist, so the verbal reasoning and analytical writing scores are not very helpful for gauging economics ability. Second, only the quantitative reasoning GRE scores (and back in the day, the scores from the analytical reasoning section before it got replaced by the analytical writing section) have been shown to be predictive of success in the coursework part of the Ph.D. program (Athey et al. 2007), so to the extent that you can only become a card-carrying Ph.D. economist if you pass these courses, the admissions committee is interested in those scores.

There may be a few departments or perhaps some random readers of your application who are interested in your verbal reasoning and analytical writing scores. These are the rare economists, usually working in applied microeconomics or economic history or sitting in heterodox departments, who think that writing and being articulate are important to being a good economist. But in general, the odds of that happening are smaller than the odds of the complete works of Karl Marx being on your reading list for graduate microeconomics, and a high verbal reasoning score can't save you from the draconian first cut based on the quantitative reasoning scores.

What does this mean for you? It means that you can't afford to take the GRE cold. It means that you should probably spend a few weeks or possibly a few months studying for the GRE and taking practice exams, and that you should focus on doing well on the quantitative reasoning section. By the way, retaking the GRE exams more than once is a really bad signal to the committee. You can probably retake them once and give some weak excuse about almost dying from flesh-eating bacteria during your first attempt; after that, though, they'll think you're just a very bad liar. So, take the GREs seriously, perhaps more seriously than any other part of your application: above all else, you want to make sure that your application gets read by a human being, and the only way to ensure this is to nail the GREs.

Coursework

Moving on to the second set of characteristics of successful candidates, we come to grades and coursework. Let's face it, the days of economics as verbal discourse in the form of *The Wealth of Nations* or *A General Theory of Unemployment* are over. Economics, for better or worse, has become a highly mathematical discipline, and you need to have and show that you have the mathematical training to make it through the program and be a well-trained economist.

For this reason, among all the courses that you take in your college career—from economics to art history—the only courses and course grades that matter for your admissions prospects are your mathematics and statistics courses, and distantly, your economics courses, but only the technical ones like game theory, mathematical economics, and econometric theory. Art history may make you a more interesting human being, but sad to say, admissions directors do not want to pick out interesting human beings; they want to select economists.

Now, you may say, well, the kind of economics that Professor L does is not math-intensive, and I want to do that kind of economics; so do I really need the math? And the answer is yes. Yes, because you still need to pass the first-year courses and exams, and they are always and everywhere highly mathematical. And yes, because behind all the easily understandable results that we read about in blogs is at least a moderate amount of technical training that you don't read about in blogs and that allows us to defensibly generate these results.

If you read the glossy brochures put out by the departments, they may mention something about math and give some examples of courses that they recommend you take, like linear algebra. Don't believe them. For the top departments, you will need much stronger mathematics and statistics training than these brochures suggest. At a minimum, to be a competitive candidate, you should have taken, beyond multivariable calculus, a year-long real analysis sequence, a course in probability theory, a course in mathematical statistics, and an advanced course in linear algebra (the kind you get in an abstract algebra sequence, not the kind that focuses on the mechanics of matrix computation). If you have more than that, all the better, and it would be great if you had majored in physics or math. Having taken these courses and having done well in them is not only a strong signal that you have the technical skills to get through the program, but will also make your first year in grad school a quintillion (10^{18}) times easier.

I should mention that the coursework and course grade standards may be lower for lower-ranked departments and for more diverse departments, especially those focused on applied topics. For these departments, you don't need to have been the top grade-getter in your real analysis course or to have taken measure theory or have majored in physics. But it helps to show that you are aware of the kind of math that is required for graduate economics by taking these courses, and it helps to show that you did reasonably well in them (no Cs—or if you did get a C, retake the course for a better grade).

And what about economics courses? Truthfully, majoring in economics is not really all that helpful for your admissions prospects. This is true for two reasons. First, knowing who does well in undergraduate economics is not terribly helpful in identifying who will be a good academic economist. Unlike other fields such as chemistry or physics, what happens in undergraduate courses bears little relation to what happens in graduate courses. For this reason, the committee cannot predict how well you will do as an academic economist based on your doing well in your undergraduate econ courses. Consequently, they don't give too much weight to your stellar performance in the usual undergraduate classes.

Undergraduate economics courses are mostly "too easy" as preparation for graduate school because these courses also need to accommodate the students who are not going to be Ph.D. economists. As it happens, this is the majority of undergrads warming the classroom seats. Most students who study economics will not get Ph.D.s in economics; they will go to law school or be consultants or investment bankers, leading placid comfortable lives while you toil away on your research. These happy many are the clientele of the undergraduate classes, and the faculty who teach these classes and are on the admissions committee know this, so they know that these economics classes are fairly useless signals of your ability.

Having said that, even though doing well in undergraduate economics courses tells the committee nothing about your academic ability, doing badly in these classes sends them a very bad signal. It's a little like using silverware when you eat. If you eat with silverware, it just means you're a regular Joe (Jill); but if you eat mashed potatoes with your fingers, people will start to wonder. So, don't eat mashed potatoes with your fingers, and do well in your mainstream economics courses to show that, at a minimum, you understand the intuition of economics. But don't think that this will get you through the graduate admissions door.

The second reason that majoring in economics won't necessarily help you in graduate school is that it won't give you the preparation you need to succeed in grad school or as an academic economist. We may rail at how mathematicized and irrelevant economics has become, and how economists have all become pointy-headed geeks out of touch with the real world, but it is a fact not easily challenged that you need to be fairly competent in math to succeed in this profession. You don't need to live in a Banach space (whatever that is) but if you can't pull As or Bs in freshman calculus, you may need to reassess whether economics is the right home for you.

I don't want to be one of those meanies who tells you that if you don't get As in real analysis, or if you don't even know what real analysis is, you should reconsider your career objectives and your deep burning desire to be an economist. But I *will* be one of those pragmatists who says that there is no avoiding math in the profession. That's the way it is. When you're grown up and armed with your Ph.D., you will get your chance to change the profession, but for now, you have to live within its constraints.

So the upshot is, in terms of undergraduate coursework, take a lot of math-based economics classes and take a lot of math and statistics classes. Oh, and do well in these classes. But you knew that.

Recommendation Letters

Letters matter, but this doesn't mean that you have to spend your undergraduate academic career kissing up to professors. In fact, don't kiss up: it's transparent to the professors, who have seen all forms of brown-nosing hundreds of times, and frankly, it is kind of demeaning to you and will annoy your classmates.

There are two things that stand out in a letter of recommendation. First, the writer is someone whom the committee knows and thinks well of as an economist. This means that it helps you a lot if you do your undergraduate work at a good research university. That's right: students at obscure universities, average state universities, and most liberal arts colleges (with some exceptions like Swarthmore and Williams) are at a disadvantage in getting the kind of letter that admissions committees in top departments want.

Now, don't get me wrong: you can get a lot from going to these places; you can become a truly educated person and a better human being. But in terms of the letter of recommendation, it can hurt you a bit. If you are fortunate enough to be at a good research university with a fair number of well-respected economists, you should take their classes and/or become a research assistant for them. Not only will you learn a lot, but they will also get to know you, and you will at least have the opportunity to earn a letter from a well-regarded economist.

And what can you do if you went to Obscure U? There are a couple of things you may want to consider aside from transferring or going back in time, which seems exceptionally difficult. First, work hard and try to be the very top student in that department. Some graduate programs—especially those ranked between 15 and 40—know that they can't attract the very best candidates, but they can get very good students who are overlooked in the admissions pool. These departments, and on occasion, some of the top departments, may accept students who are at the very top at their lesser-known universities. A slightly lower-ranked graduate program may make you a very good offer and invest a great deal in you, giving you more attention than you would receive if you went to a bigger-deal department.

Second, even if your university is obscure, there may be one or two prominent economists in the department. You should try to take their classes, work for them, and get to know them. Ideally, they will do research in your field of interest, but even if their interests don't align with yours, you can still learn a lot from working for them.

Third, spend a summer or two working as an intern or research assistant for a well-known economist at another university. Write a fan letter asking Professor Famous Economist if you can work for him. Bear in mind that he will get other fan letters (although let's be frank, not that many), mainly from students at his own Famous University, but if you can sell yourself, he just might take you on.

A related and possibly better alternative, if you have time, is to be a full-time research assistant for a couple of years for Professor Famous Economist, or at a serious economic research center like the National Bureau of Economic Research or the Research Department of a major Federal Reserve Bank (Chicago, Minneapolis, New York, and San Francisco are some good ones). Many very good economists work at or are consultants at these centers, and in working with them you will have the opportunity to pick up a lot of useful research skills in addition to a recommendation letter.

I should also mention, in the interest of completeness, that the reputation of the letter writer within the economics profession as a whole is less of an issue if you are primarily targeting mid-ranked or lower-ranked departments. While a letter from Professor Famous Economist would of course be helpful (unless he writes you a terrible one—see my next point below), what is most helpful in non-top-ranked departments is to have a recommendation letter from someone who is known and respected in the particular field of economics in which you wish to specialize. Not all economists who do excellent work in their subfields are in the tippy-top departments; in fact, a great many are not. Since in academia pretty much everyone knows or at least knows *of* everyone else working in their subfield (I am not kidding), you should try to have your letters written by economists—preferably tenured at the associate or full professor level—doing research in your field of interest. For lower-ranked programs, letters from these economists will credibly inform other economists that you are suited to be a Ph.D. student in (that subfield of) economics.

Aside from the scholarly status of the letter writer, an important aspect of a letter of recommendation is that it says something positive about you. While you can't have total control over this, you can have *some* control. By this I mean, you can work your butt off to impress the letter writer. As I mentioned earlier, blatant kissing up is tacky and ineffective. What is inoffensive and effective is working really hard and doing a really good job. You may be out of luck if a professor is someone who is stingy with his praise or difficult to please (although the admissions committee will likely know this about the letter writer), but in general, doing a good job for your professor should be enough to get a helpful letter from him or her.

Research Experience

Serious research experience while you are an undergraduate or for several years after you have graduated sends a good signal to admissions committees. It shows that you were interested enough in serious economics to seek out research experience, that you learned research skills that you can bring to bear in your own research, and that you know what you are getting into.

For research experience to be most useful for your chances of admission, the kind of research experience you had should match the kind of research you state that you want to do in your application. So it doesn't help you much if you say, hey, look at me, I spent all this time working with Stata®, but it made me realize I want to do theory. You should show that you can do at least the rudiments of whatever it is you want to do.

Seriousness of Intellectual Purpose

As you may have already seen in your college days, there are many ambitious undergraduates. There are some people who are ambitious because they are competitive and just like to be at the top of the heap with whatever they are doing; and then there are people who are ambitious because they really care about what they are doing. You want to be among the latter, and you want to show that you care about the intellectual work that you are about to undertake.

While people who are ambitious for its own sake or who just enjoy the rewards that come from being on top will do well in graduate school and in life, the low pay and meager perks of the academy mean that it best suits people who really care about their research topic and would do research even if they weren't being paid to do it.

So, do some introspection and find your real purpose. If you can't get super excited about economic research, then consider doing something else. Take that burning ambition and apply it to some other field that you can get excited about, and you will succeed in that other area. But don't apply to graduate school just because it's something that you're good at but don't really care much about.

If you want to succeed, both in the admissions process in economics and as a Ph.D. economist, find that seriousness of intellectual purpose. And show that seriousness in the courses that you choose to take, the assiduousness with which you work in those courses, the research experiences you choose to have, and some introspection about your own research agenda.

The Personal Statement

Economists are not known to be good writers, so you may not be very excited about writing your personal statement. The good news is that economists are typically also terrible readers—by which I mean, they dislike spending their time reading. Consequently, your personal statement will get less than two minutes of reading time, and elegant prose is by no means required. Because of the stacks of applicant files the committee must move through, you, your file, and your essay will barely be remembered unless you are a superstar or you come off as a major-league jerk in your essay. Trust me, the most anyone remembers is: did undergrad at College S, interested in macro, and my colleague P wrote a letter for her. So, first, don't sweat the writing too much: just write simply and don't make obvious errors.

The second thing to remember is that unlike the college personal statement, which is designed to show how interesting a person you are, the graduate school personal statement is designed to show how scholarly and serious a person you are. It helps to have something idiosyncratic so that people remember you, but oddly enough, having had a cool experience like the Peace Corps may actually work against you (unless you are studying economic development), because most economists lead pretty boring lives and are wholly unimpressed with such experiences as signals of how good an economist you will be.

So take the personal statement as an opportunity to clarify your research interests. Be as detailed as you can. If you have been working on a specific research project, write about it, but you will want to show your essay to your professors, or to TAs or grad students you know, to be sure that your ambitions are not overly broad or so non-mainstream as to be viewed as unrealistic. A big mistake made in these personal statements is that they overreach or are insufficiently scholarly, suggesting that the applicant does not really know what he is getting into intellectually.

In addition, you should know that the committee wants to put you into a bin—applied microeconomics, industrial organization, international trade—and it's your job in your personal statement to tell them which bin to put you in. Your bin determines which faculty members will read your application and which faculty members the admission committee thinks you want to work with. If you express an interest in an area where no faculty in the department are working, this could derail your application. So, be specific (choose only one or two bins) so that you don't look unfocused and undisciplined, and focus on the areas that, in addition to being of interest to you, are also strengths of that department (yes, this may mean writing a slightly different statement for each department).

Unlike in other disciplines, where the personal statement is used to evaluate your ability to write and communicate well, in economics it is used just to state some relevant facts about yourself. The good news is that you need not worry about being eloquent or interesting (although a clear, well-written essay is always a joy to read); you can just focus on stating your interests and showing that you have thought seriously about them and are ready to embark on a research career.

And be careful and sparing with the personal details. Sappy stories about your life are to be avoided unless you can tell a compelling narrative about why being cut from the junior varsity basketball team crystallized your decision to study dynamic models with heterogeneous agents.

Economics Department Rankings

We live in a world obsessed with rankings. And there is no shortage of lists that numerically rank economics departments. There is the *U.S. News & World Report* annual list, the National Research Council rankings, the RepEc rankings, the studies by Grijalva and Nowell (2008) and Kalaitzidakis, Mamuneas, and Stengos (2003) to name only a few.

How should you use these rankings to guide where you should apply? Some applicants simply want to go to the most prestigious program they can get into and take a shotgun approach, applying to all of the top schools regardless of how well the departments suit their interests or personality. Other applicants take a more conservative route and selectively choose schools on the basis of how the departments fare in their area of interest, whether there is a superstar professor with whom they want to work, whether the university suits their geographic or lifestyle preferences, or whether it's close to where their girlfriend wants to be.

I used to have an opinion about this, but I have since learned that people value what they value. Which is another way of saying *de gustibus non est disputandum*: there's no arguing about taste. Students' preferences vary a great deal, and as long as you are clear on what yours are, any number of approaches can be optimal.

Many students think that where you go to school affects your initial job placement, so it's crucial to go to the best department that you can regardless of how well it suits you.[1] This is more or less true, but the situation is more complex than it would first seem. It is true that the number of graduates produced by Ph.D. programs is far greater than the number they hire. Thus, graduates from top Ph.D. programs will be placed in departments further down the chain, pushing graduates of lower-ranked departments even lower in their placements.

At the same time, how your graduate institution affects your placement is more complicated than this. First, placement relationships between institutions are based on personal relationships between professors. The kinds of people your advisor knows and which departments they are in could mean that some departments are more accessible to you than others. If your professor knows a lot of faculty members at another institution—because he went to graduate school there, has placed previous students there, or has a collaborator or friend there—this increases your chance of at least getting an initial interview there. These other institutions, however, can be of higher or lower rank than your home institution.

Because of the idiosyncrasies of personal relationships, having an advisor in a highly ranked department will not necessarily help you be placed at the highest-ranked institution you might be capable of.

Another thing to consider is that not all top-ranked departments have stellar placement records. Amir and Knauff (2008) construct a ranking based on how well economics departments place their students, an ordering which may perhaps be more useful for applicants than a generic *U.S. News & World Report* ranking.

But bear in mind that if you are a low-ranked student at a top program, you may well have a worse graduate school experience in terms of how your fellow graduate students and the faculty view you and treat you. While going to a high-prestige department may score you points on the social scene outside the department, within the department you will be judged *relative* to your peers, and you may well feel socially isolated and be given far fewer resources (such as research support and advisor attention) than you would have had if you had gone to a lower-ranked institution and positioned yourself higher in the student distribution. In many lower-ranked departments, there is a great deal of investment directed toward the top students, so you would probably get a better education there. And, empirically, the top students at Minnesota and Michigan have been placed in higher-ranking departments than students in the bottom third of the distribution at Harvard and MIT.

Of course, no one anticipates going into a program and being at the bottom of their class. But I make this point to highlight the importance of the match between you and the department. If you are not highly technical, or perhaps you work best with a fair amount of guidance, or you find the grad students in certain departments a little too nerdy, you may well feel (and be) neglected if you set your sights on the highest-ranking departments.

By the way, a good measure of where the department thinks you fit in the student distribution is the financial package they offer you (of course, this only holds true in departments where offers vary; some departments have a rule of giving all admitted candidates the same offer). If the department offers you a competitive stipend, they think you will do pretty well; if it offers you tuition only, they don't think highly of your prospects. Of course, I would not over-interpret these offers as a measure of your own worth; you have private information about your own abilities, motivation, and work habits, and you may just prove them wrong, but these offers give you a measure of where the department thinks you stand.

Notwithstanding *de gustibus non est disputandum*, I do have two specific pieces of advice in terms of where to apply. First, if you have a rather limited budget, identify the departments that are the best match *ex ante* (i.e., before applying) in terms of faculty and department specialization, and focus your applications on these. It helps a great deal if you or your advisor know and have relationships with specific faculty members in these departments. If, however, money is no object, then apply to as many departments as you can (top-ranked and middle-ranked, as well lower-ranked safety schools in locations where you wouldn't mind living for five or six years), and determine *ex post* (i.e., after acceptance) how well you would fit in, when you go for the campus visit.

A second rule of thumb is that, in general, going to a bigger department is probably better than going to a small department. Faculty leave, students change their minds about their areas of interest, many things can happen in the course of your graduate education, and you do not want to be left adrift if the only professor you wanted to work with decamps for another department.

A final word about rankings. Despite the glut of rankings and all the different dimensions along which departments may be ranked, what these rankings *don't* tell you is that University M handholds its students, University H attracts the superstars but also has some real underperformers that it shuttled through from undergrad, and University C can't advise its students out of a paper bag.

The problem with rankings, of course, is that they tell you how life is *for the professors* and where they sit in the pecking order of the profession; they don't tell you what life will be like for you as a graduate student. Now if all you are concerned about is the status and bragging rights of your department, then you should pay attention to the rankings, especially the *U.S. News & World Report* rankings, which are based largely on reputation and halo effects.

Some students would rather pass up a higher-status school for a place that has friendlier and more accessible faculty. Others don't mind being left alone and would rather go to a highly ranked school even if they are treated like lint by the famous faculty members. Some students would rather go to a lesser-ranked school where there are lots of faculty specializing in their subfield than go to a better overall school that has only one person in their subfield. And some students would not be caught dead as a grad student in a city of less than a million people even if they could be in a far better program somewhere in the sticks.

If you have strong status preferences, then rankings will give you a good measure of relative status. Rankings can also help you if you are already clear that you want to go into policy or the private sector (although I would suggest rereading Chapter 1 if you already know this is what you want to do). In these sectors, there is a continuing high value—both professionally and socially—in where you got your Ph.D. These places don't much care about where your dissertation fits into the larger economic literature; they want you to use your analytical brainpower to solve their clients' problems now. For these places, given that you are able to do the work, the highest-status departments—which is to say, those that will most impress their clients—will probably give you the highest returns.

If, however, you are concerned about your day-to-day experience as a graduate student and your job placement, then frankly, rankings don't tell you much. You are better off going online and posting in a graduate school forum, or asking junior faculty or graduate students at your university what the rap is on the different departments; or better yet, visiting the departments yourself and asking the students there.

Frequently Asked Questions

I am interested in policy. Should I take a policy job before graduate school?

No. While I commend your interest in policy, I would recommend that you mention nothing at all about this interest in your application. While it is true that many economists eventually work for the government and play a very important role in policy, you as an applicant will be, sad to say, considered less intellectually rigorous if you mention that you are interested in policy. The only exception might be if you say that you are deeply interested in arcane aspects of monetary policy.

I encourage you to harbor a *secret* interest in policy until you get accepted and, even then, reveal yourself only to your trusted friends and advisors. Your main goal should be to convey (and actually hold) an interest in heavy-duty economics, and if you can apply economic theory to policy, all the better, but your main commitment is to the intellectual project of economics.

The only exception to this no-policy-job-before-grad-school rule is if you are able to get a position at a policy institution that has many good academic economists and that is known for its serious economic analysis of policy. Examples include the Council of Economic Advisors and the Research Departments of some Federal Reserve Banks (see my discussion in the "Recommendation Letters" section of this chapter). Working in these policy jobs is basically similar to being a research assistant to some Professor Famous Economist, and you want to make sure that you are developing your research skills (as well as getting to know the very good academic economists who consult or work there).

If you find yourself taking a policy job prior to graduate school—either because this is the only position available to you or you are just really interested in policy—you should, in your application, focus on the research aspects of this policy job and the kinds of skills you learned in this job (statistical analysis, computing, etc.). You should also make sure that you have other credentials, such as coursework, that show your technical competencies.

I love teaching and am really interested in teaching (as well as research). Should I mention this in my application?

In general, no. Although some faculty may be interested in and supportive of your teaching aspirations, an interest in teaching is unfortunately considered to be a signal of a less (academically) serious applicant. If you have teaching experience, you should feel free to mention this, although you might want to focus on how teaching led you to, say, be more curious about certain aspects of economic research.

How important is the college I went to, and how important is networking?

Where you went to school affects your application in three ways. First, good schools attract good students, and so if the admissions director knows nothing about you except where you went to school, she will assume you are an average graduate of that school, and the average graduate from a good school is generally better prepared than the average student from a less good school.

Second, good schools offer good courses and good opportunities to do research. So if you went to a good school, people will assume you got good preparation or at least had the opportunity to have had good preparation.

Finally, as I mentioned above, going to a good school puts you in contact with prominent economists who can write you credible letters. This is the "who you know" effect.

Of these three factors, the last one is probably the most important. Economists whom others know as being able to discern good economists, and with whom they have long-term professional relationships, can be trusted to send true signals of their students.

This means that even a ho-hum letter from a credible economist can trump an enthusiastic letter from someone no one knows. As I mentioned earlier, however, even if you didn't go to a good school, you can make some constructive efforts to remedy this deficit.

The reason the first two factors are less important is that, if the admissions director and the admissions committee are experienced enough, they will know the range of courses that are available at your university. If they see that you didn't take the hard courses, or got Bs while other applicants got As, they will downgrade you very quickly. In this way, not doing so well at a good school can hurt you in the graduate admissions process. Going to Harvard may help you pick up girls in bars, but it won't get you very far when people have your mediocre transcript *and* have other applicants' transcripts as well.

The long and the short of it is that educational pedigree, where you went to school, matters, but not in quite the way you might think.

Should I try to publish before graduate school?

Yes. Try to publish before graduate school, during graduate school, and after graduate school. But do not publish indiscriminately; where you publish does matter. For starters, although blogging is tempting to do and easy to break into, think carefully before you put up a blog post. The possibility of saying something provocative that annoys somebody on some economics faculty somewhere, or of making some cute claim that can be distorted out of context, is non-negligible, and the potential downside (at this stage in your professional life) is immense. Focus your time on scholarly work; while an op-ed in the *New York Times* may up your coolness factor by a smidge, too many op-eds before graduate school gives the impression that you are too diffuse or superficial intellectually, that you do not know what scholarly writing entails, or worse, that you are more interested in attention than in scholarship. If you are serious about an academic career, you should try to publish (only) in scholarly journals that are peer reviewed. There will be time enough to sit back, stroke your beard, and write op-eds after you have finished your Ph.D.

And Finally . . .

Remember that, although graduate school is where you will prepare yourself intellectually for a life as an academic economist, it is also where you will meet interesting people and make good friends. When deciding where to apply and which offer to accept, not only will you want to figure out where you will do your best learning and which departments will best place you; you will also want to find out which programs will suit you best socially. For five or six years, your fellow students will commiserate with you through exams, read your papers, and celebrate your achievements. After graduation, when everyone has dispersed, you will look forward to seeing them at professional meetings. You may even coauthor with them. Although you may have collegial relationships in the departments where you work as a Ph.D. economist, the relationships that you build in graduate school tend to be more personal and longer-lived than the professional relationships you build in your workplace. So be socially observant when you go on your site visits, and be sure to confirm for yourself that the grad students there are people with whom you would want to be friends for a long time to come.

Graduate school is an important step in your professional career as an academic. Your objective in your application should be to show that you are prepared for graduate school and that you know and value what is important to Ph.D. economists, especially the Ph.D. economist who is the admissions director. With a bit of savvy and a bit of luck, there will be a program among the many that accept you that will be just what you want and need.

Notes

1. Some may argue that good placement may be more a function of selection than added value. In other words, Harvard and MIT place their students

well, not because they train their students better but because they get the top students. For the graduate school applicant, however, the mechanism through which good placement happens is a second order concern relative to the fact of a good placement record itself.

References

Amir, Rabah, and Malgorzata Knauff. 2008. "Ranking Economics Departments Worldwide on the Basis of Ph.D. Placement." *Review of Economics and Statistics* 90: 185–190.

Athey, Susan, Lawrence F. Katz, Alan B. Krueger, Steven Levitt, and James Poterba. 2007. "What Does Performance in Graduate School Predict?" *American Economics Review Papers and Proceedings* 97: 512–518.

Grijalva, Therese C., and Clifford Nowell. 2008. "A Guide to Graduate Study in Economics: Ranking Economics Departments by Fields of Expertise." *Southern Economic Journal* 74: 971–976.

Kalaitzidakis, Pantelis, Theofanis P. Mamuneas, and Thanasis Stengos. 2003. "Rankings of Academic Journals and Institutions in Economics." *Journal of the European Economic Association* 1: 1346–1366.

Further Reading

Colander, David. 2007. *The Making of an Economist Redux*. Princeton, N.J.: Princeton University Press.

Klamer, Arjo, and David Colander. 1990. *The Making of an Economist*. Boulder, Colo.: Westview Press.

Useful Web Pages

Advice from Famous Economists

- Susan Athey: http://kuznets.harvard.edu/~athey/gradadv.html
- Greg Mankiw: Advice for Students section at http://gregmankiw.blog spot.com
- Jeff Smith: http://www-personal.umich.edu/~econjeff/Courses/Advice%20on%20Graduate%20School%20in%20Economics%200911.pdf

American Economic Association

- Graduate Study in Economics page: http://www.aeaweb.org/grad students/
- List of U.S. graduate programs: http://www.aeaweb.org/gradstudents/Schools.php
- Rankings of graduate programs: http://www.aeaweb.org/gradstudents/Rankings.php

Online Forums (use at your own risk—lots of misinformation here)

- Test Magic Urch Forum: http://www.urch.com/forums/phd-economics/

Chapter 3

Getting Through First Year: Welcome to Boot Camp

There is nothing like the first year in graduate school. And we should be very, very glad of this. The first year of a doctoral program is universally considered the worst year of a graduate student's life. There are a couple of reasons why this is the case. First, there is absolutely no leeway in the courses that you are required to take. Despite the diversity of economics departments across the United States, virtually every economist-in-training is required to take microeconomics, macroeconomics, and econometrics in his first year. This means that there is at least one course and possibly two that you will dislike because they are not terribly related to your personal area of interest. If you like microeconomic theory, then you might think macroeconomics and econometrics are a waste of time. If you are an empiricist, then you will wonder why you are spending all your time proving theorems. Of course, you may truly love learning for its own sake and may want to learn everything that is presented to you, and this is laudable, but because time is so scarce in the first year, you may still grow deeply resentful of the time you have to spend working on problem sets that are not at all related to what you want to do your research on.

Which leads me to the second reason first year is so arduous. There is, simply put, a lot of work. Typically, there is a problem set due for each class every week, and the work is time-consuming. If you have never seen the material before, it is challenging to learn it all, not to mention master it all, and you simply have to put in the hours if you want to do well. Again, you may resent this and mourn the loss of your free time, your relationships, your mental and physical well-being, your intellectual breadth. Moreover, since the material is new and difficult, you may feel that you're already putting in a lot of time and effort but still doing badly, and this will make you feel worse about yourself and your direction.

Third, there is the intellectual challenge of working on the same kind of thing day in and day out. This is perhaps more of a difficulty for American students, who have had undergraduate training at institutions where there is an emphasis on a broad liberal arts education. In graduate school, you are required to focus with great intensity on one subject, and many students find this focus constraining and boring. In economic-speak, there may well be diminishing returns. There may also be something to the fact that, once you are in the sausage factory and see how the sausage is made, you are no longer interested in having anything to do with economic sausages.

Fourth, if you have chosen to go to the best graduate program that you can get into, the competition is tougher. Presumably, if you have decided to get a Ph.D. and have successfully gained entry, you would have done well in your courses as an undergraduate. There is selection among the top undergraduates to go on to graduate programs, so in graduate programs there are just more good students with whom you will have to contend. Even if you attended an elite undergraduate college, there will be a greater number of smart people in the graduate program, and it's harder to do as well as you have been doing. If you are used to being at the top of the class, you will find that it's much more difficult to attain the same relative ranking. Because of this inevitable decline in your relative status, your ego will take a beating.

Finally, because of all of the points I mentioned above, you will feel that you are doing badly, not enjoying yourself, losing aspects of your life that you want back, and profoundly lacking in interest in substantial parts of your work. You will then start to doubt yourself and your decision. Perhaps you will see some of your friends making money in real-world jobs and enjoying their weekends instead of worrying about problem sets. You may wonder if pursuing a Ph.D. is what you should be doing, and whether you belong in graduate school and in the profession. In a vicious cycle, this kind of self-doubt leads to even worse performance.

Sounds like fun, no? No one ever talks about these first-year stresses on Prospective Student Day, except perhaps if you happen to encounter a first-year student in a particularly indiscreet moment (although in general, schools wisely try to keep first-year graduate students away from their prospective students). But have no doubt: the first year of an economics program is one of the most intellectually demanding and emotionally demanding years of the graduate program and possibly, to be slightly overly dramatic, your life.

Now that we've got that out of the way, what do we do? A helpful metaphor may be the following. First year is often compared to military boot camp. And in some ways, it is boot camp. You are asked to go through an intensive period of extremely demanding work. If you complete it, you will presumably be stronger and more competent than you were before you entered. But boot camp can be so difficult that some people crack under the pressure; they feel overwhelmed and they leave, or if they choose to stay, they become a different person, and not in a good way. But there are many who remain and thrive, who learn the system and learn to do well within the system, who learn what they need to learn but remain grounded and sure of themselves. You want to be one of these people.

Now, like military boot camp and other difficult activities that you have to endure, the more you know about what is in store for you, the better off you will be. Of course, no amount of simply reading about something will take the place of experiencing it, but to maximize your chances of succeeding, you must be psychologically prepared. And to be prepared, you should learn as much as you can about what will take place. That is the purpose of this chapter: to give you an overview of the structure of the first year, to describe the emotional and intellectual challenges you will face, and to give you some strategies for coping with these challenges. The goal is to give you what you need so that you come out on the other side of boot camp a personal and intellectual success.

The Structure and Substance of the First Year

Despite the large variation in focus, methodological emphasis, and culture across economics departments in the United States, there is astonishing uniformity in what is taught in the first year of a graduate economics program. First year will consist of three full-year courses: microeconomics, macroeconomics, and econometrics. There may be courses in addition to these three, and in business school and public policy graduate programs, macroeconomics coursework may be a bit more limited, but for the most part, these three courses form the core of the first year.

While most of you already know the substantive differences between micro, macro, and 'metrics from your undergraduate courses, it may be useful to do a quick overview of the content of the graduate versions of these courses. In first year, graduate microeconomics consists of consumer theory, producer theory, general equilibrium theory, and game theory. In other words, in economics there are two types of agents, consumers and producers, and you learn first about how economists model individual consumer behavior, then how economists model individual producer behavior, what the system looks like when you put all the consumers and producers together and they act as atomistic agents (general equilibrium), and finally what the system looks like when you put all the agents together and they act strategically (game theory).

You may have noticed that there is a lot of theory in graduate microeconomics (consumer *theory*, producer *theory*, general equilibrium *theory*, game *theory*). Actually, all of the first-year courses are really about theory, even econometrics. And what theory means in the economics world is formal (mathematical) stories about how people and firms (and governments and data points) behave. One consequence of this formal theory-based curriculum is that these courses consist of making sparse assumptions and mathematically proving statements (theorems) using these assumptions. This comes as a surprise to many students, but is really the fundamental core of first-year economics training.

Turning to macroeconomics, there is a bit more heterogeneity in macroeconomics courses across different economics departments, and even among different professors within the same department. That said, virtually all departments teach the same *methods*. You are taught methods to deal with both continuous-time and discrete-time dynamic problems. The rest of the time, you are taught a random assortment of models, which vary in their breadth and depth and emphasis, depending on the idiosyncratic preferences of the professors teaching your particular course. These include growth models, models of money, models of labor and search, to name a few. Depending on which department you are in, you get different doses of neoclassical and neo-Keynesian models. To underscore my point about the diversity of the graduate macroeconomics curriculum, whereas there seems to be convergence on the standard graduate microeconomics theory text (Mas-Colell, Whinston, and Green 1995), there has been no convergence whatsoever on a standard graduate macro theory text. In my opinion, this lack of convergence reflects the state of affairs with macroeconomics research and macro knowledge in general, but I will save that diatribe for another day and book.

An important point to note is that the gulf between under-graduate macroeconomics courses and graduate macroeconomics courses is approximately twice the size of the Atlantic Ocean. In undergraduate courses, the emphasis is on intuition and how to interpret changes in broad economic indicators, like inflation, GDP, and employment. In graduate courses, the focus is primarily on developing competence in mathematical methods, proving properties of something called policy functions, and specifying assumptions and conditions under which certain properties in a system hold. Most students bemoan the void in intuition in macroeconomics courses. In modern macro, the emphasis is on theory. There is some empirical work, but because there are simply far less macroeconomic data to work with relative to microeconomic data (there are more individuals than there are countries), the empirical and data parts of macroeconomics are de-emphasized.

Finally, there is the econometrics sequence. You may think, finally, a class with concrete applications! Not so fast. The graduate econometrics sequence is rarely about statistical applications to data. In fact, it is entirely possible (likely) that you will go through the entire year without knowing how to run a statistical package. (All the more reason for getting this experience prior to graduate school.) Again, the emphasis is on theory, this time econometric and statistical theory.

Graduate econometrics is typically broken down into three components. The first section is probability and mathematical statistical theory. This material establishes the foundation for the study of subsequent, more specialized methods, and often overlaps with a good undergraduate mathematical statistics course. A second section focuses on econometric theory and methods related to microeconomic data, where there are many observations but perhaps not many time periods. And a third section focuses on theory and methods related to macroeconomic data, where there are not many observations but usually long time periods. Again, the focus is on theory and deriving properties of things called estimators.

Prior to the first year, there is often a month-long math camp (in some programs there are longer math camps, extending through the first semester of the first year). In math camp, students are exposed to the mathematical concepts and tools that they will be expected to use in the first year of graduate school. These methods include optimization techniques, basic concepts of real analysis, linear algebra, an overview of mathematical statistics, and a brief exposure to the Hamiltonian and Bellman techniques.

In my experience, not much is accomplished during the short version of math camp (the version that runs just several weeks instead of a full semester). For those who have seen the techniques before, it is a complete review and waste of time. For students who have not been exposed to the techniques, the topics go by too quickly and superficially for a good understanding of the material. The consensus seems to be that, even though math camp is not a cognitively useful way to spend time for any subset of students, it does provide a good excuse to get to know your new classmates. A second by-product is that it exposes students who have not seen the techniques to mathematical tools that will be used in the first year so that, at a minimum, the students don't freak out when they see them (this does not mean, however, that they will actually know how to use the tools). The cynical justification for the short version of math camp is that it absolves the faculty of any obligation to help students with the details of solving problems since the faculty can say that method X or Y has already been covered in math camp. The upshot is, if you know the material, there are probably better uses of your time, but it does provide a pretext for some pre-term socializing.

Who Does Well in the First Year

The purpose of the first year is to intellectually socialize you into being an economist. Regardless of specialization, an educated economist is expected to know the basic theory and methods outside of his special field. So if you're a theoretical macroeconomist, you are still expected to know something about microeconomics and econometrics. If you're an econometrician, you still need to know economic theory.

I call this the Great Books approach to economic education. In college education, the Great Books approach assumes that there is a fixed set of ideas or texts with which every educated person should be familiar. While this approach is controversial as educational theory, it raises very few eyebrows within economics. This is so because, whereas there is very little agreement on the various and sundry things that every generally educated person should know, there is a great deal of consensus on the core content of economics. One implication of this consensus and this way of educating economists is that, regardless of where you go for your Ph.D., you will be taught the same things (with some variation in whether you are given a more or less in-depth treatment, and how close the content is to the research frontier). A much broader implication is that every economist will be able to talk shop with every other economist, and most economists will agree on how an Economist would approach a particular problem. This gives economics an apparent unifying quality that few other disciplines have (which makes us envied or hated or both). Of course, research within economics has become so specialized that it is unlikely that you will be able to drop in on any seminar and follow everything, but more likely than not, unless the presenter is hopelessly incompetent, you should be able to follow the presentation at least on a superficial level and understand where the material fits within economics.

The reason for this digression on ye olde Great Books is to emphasize the educational purpose of the first year. The goal of the first year is to make you a well-rounded economist and to show you the fundamental technical skills that you will need when you further specialize.[1] As you go through your first year, it is important to not lose sight of this teaching objective. The breadth of the first year means that there are likely to be some areas that you dislike or in which you will do poorly, and that you may feel overwhelmed by the many disparate topics and models that you are expected to master. This is okay and completely expected.

So who are the students who tend to do well the first year? The single best predictor of good performance during the first year is whether a student has seen and studied the material before. This point may seem silly and obvious. Clearly, if someone has learned previously how to take matrix derivatives, she will be better at differentiating matrices than someone who is learning it for the first time. And yet, many first-year students beat themselves up for not doing well relative to their classmates, when in fact many of their classmates have already seen the material found in the first year. This prior exposure explains why many students who were educated overseas do much better during the first year of grad school than those educated in the United States. Unlike American students, whose liberal arts educations have been by design more broad than deep, most international students come from undergraduate programs that focused entirely on economics, so they are at a more advanced level of technical proficiency at the end of their college days. In addition, and this may be a trade secret, but the standard for graduate admissions for international students is higher than the standard for American students. The primary reason for this is that graduate programs know the quality of and faculty at American universities far better than the quality of faculty at institutions overseas. To minimize the risk surrounding the greater uncertainty of a given international candidate, graduate programs tend to accept only those international candidates with unambiguously superior credentials, such a master's degree from a well-known university or a fantastic letter from an overseas professor with an international reputation. Thus, almost all students who were educated overseas are entering Ph.D. programs *having already learned* the material taught in the first year—and in many cases the second year—of graduate economics programs. Unsurprisingly, they tend to do very well.

This prior-exposure advantage also kicks in for students who have already taken graduate-level courses. This advantage is particularly noticeable if students were undergraduates in the same institution where they are doing their graduate work. In addition to having already seen the material, they know the department's (and the professors') priorities and preferences for certain models and approaches, and they likely have copies of old problem sets and exams (more on this later).

But what if you don't fall into either category? There's no use bemoaning the terrible unfairness of it all. Many of your classmates will be better prepared than you; this is something over which you have no control. That said, what this discussion should tell you is that it is in your interest, if you have not yet applied to graduate programs, to take as many graduate economics courses as you can. I mentioned this in Chapter 2 when I discussed applications, but it is also relevant here. Not only does taking the courses and doing well help you with being admitted into a program, but it will also make your first year feel much more manageable.

A second very good predictor of performance during the first year is having taken advanced math courses, especially those requiring proofs. The ability to make sense of abstract definitions and theorems and apply them in the service of proving mathematical statements is an important skill in graduate school and in the profession in general, even if your professorial job will not involve proving things on a daily basis. For example, even if you are an applied empirical economist, you will want to be able to know and use the latest findings in econometric theory.

Students who have not taken advanced math may have a misconception that doing well in, say, calculus, or in engineering courses is a trustworthy signal of math ability. There is the view that math is about computation or following rules or being good at algebra. Certainly these skills don't hurt, but they are quite different from the kind of mathematical thinking that is helpful in economics. Being able to think abstractly and to reason with abstract objects is very important in economics. Of course, these abstract objects relate to real, concrete economic entities, which are the things that we really care about, but we work with abstract objects so that we can make general statements instead of working things out case-by-case for every scenario. For some students, this kind of abstract mathematical thinking appears very early—this is why there are five-year-old math prodigies—but for many of us, this kind of skill is developed by taking proofs-based advanced math courses such as real analysis and abstract algebra.

You may have noticed that the two most important predictors of performance in the first year of graduate school (having previously seen the material and having taken advanced math courses) relate to what you knew *before* you came to grad school, as opposed to your work ethic, creativity, or independence. While work ethic and so on are surely important for *later on* in graduate school (and in the profession), they are far less important for the first year than having previously seen the models and having previously worked with the mathematical tools required for economic analysis. In this respect, the first year is a very different animal from the rest of graduate school and the rest of your professional life.

You may think, what a bizarre way to structure a graduate program: to have first-year performance not be dependent on factors that are so important for success in the profession. And it is deeply strange. One way to think about this, though, is that technical competence, creativity, and work ethic are all necessary conditions for doing well in the profession. The first year weights technical competence heavily to the exclusion of other factors. Subsequent graduate school years give greater weight to creativity, work ethic, and independent thought. In other words, technical proficiency is the initial screen; development of other useful skills can only come after passing through the initial screen. An analogy might be that first year is about getting your driver's license. You need to show basic technical competency to receive your license. Once you have your license, you have more freedom to go out on the race course and push the limits of driving a bit.

If you are already coming into a graduate program with the advantages I've mentioned, enjoy the reprieve: you will have a greater opportunity to enjoy the first year and to push yourself to a greater understanding of the material you have seen. Bear in mind, though, that the workload may still be heavy. Problem sets need to be written up. Readings need to be done. Don't take your knowledge for granted.

If you do not have the advantages I've mentioned, the best way you can compensate for this relative lack of preparedness is to work harder. You will have to put in more hours to learn new material; it takes time and intellectual intensity to master this new content, especially when you are, in effect, given less time to do so. Don't be fooled by the bravado of your fellow classmates and don't waste your energy comparing yourself to them. You have some catching up to do. Put in the hours to do it.

Empirically, by the way, it is the case that many students who do well first year are not the students who will do well during the rest of graduate school, or indeed in the profession. First year only favors the technically prepared.

Study Strategies for First-Year Courses

I won't go into much detail about the nuts and bolts of studying except to say that studying graduate economics is not like reading history, and more importantly, it is not like studying undergraduate economics. By this I mean, it is not sufficient to read your texts, generally understand what you read, and affirm to yourself that you know what's going on. With graduate economics, the devil is in the mathematical details. You must know the definitions, theorems, and proofs cold. You will be expected to know many of these proofs and also know how to prove new statements that you've never seen before using the definitions, theorems, and proof strategies that you've already seen. You will be expected to solve, at a minimum, mathematical models that have been presented to you in lectures and to solve more sophisticated models that build on the models you've seen. And you will be expected to do so under timed conditions, either because problem sets have deadlines or because you are given limited time to complete your exams. You may consider the details a waste of time and think that you are far too busy a person to pay attention to such petty details. This would be a mistake. No one is going to ask you, "So tell me, in your own words, why are all Walrasian equilibria pareto-efficient?" Instead, they will say something like, "State and prove the First Fundamental Theorem of Welfare Economics" and then deduct points if you don't state the correct conditions. Memorize if you must, but know those petty details.

Two other study strategies are staples of graduate economics. First, join a study group, but not just any study group. Many students get into a panic during the first week of courses thinking, *I must find a study group immediately or I will fail all my classes and be a total social loser.* They either run around asking any classmate with whom they happen to strike up a conversation to be their study buddy, or they try to suss out classmates on their potential academic usefulness and then secure a study group contract with those presumed to be the smartest. I would advise against either strategy.

Although study groups have academic objectives, the most functional study groups are those whose members are compatible in other ways. The best study groups tend to form around friendship groups, or among classmates who have similar cultural or religious ties, or who are intellectually or temperamentally similar. Thus, the partiers find each other, as do the hard-core bookish types. In diverse programs, segregation also occurs along the dimensions of language and nationality.

Some students believe that the "best" study groups should be formed rationally. There should be a microeconomics expert, a macroeconomics expert, and an econometrics expert, to minimize the risk of encountering a problem that the study group cannot solve. Of course, having members of the group who compensate for each other's weaknesses is a bonus. At the same time, groups chosen solely on this basis, and not on any other personal or social connections, tend to disintegrate rather quickly at the first sign of conflict because there is nothing holding the group together.

Thus, my advice for finding a study group is to find friends first, and these people will emerge quite naturally as your study group. In the beginning, talk to everyone about both work and play to see who best clicks with you. Work with different study groups and different people to see how their style of studying meshes with your own. By the middle of the first semester, and certainly by the beginning of the second semester, study and friendship groups will have coalesced, and these groups tend to be quite stable as they are sustained by members who like and respect each other.

Some of you brainiacs may not be into the study group thing. You already know quite a bit and you can solve your own problems without anyone else's help, thank you very much. Working with others constrains you. People get on your nerves.

Now, it is possible to go through the first year as a lone ranger. But taking this route takes its toll. You lose the insurance of having someone say just the right thing to spark an idea in the unlikely event that you do not know how to solve a problem. Furthermore, you may feel socially isolated. A lot of personal connections, not just intellectual connections, are made through study group activities, and these connections can be important for your emotional health and for feeling a part of your graduate school cohort. Try to reach beyond your shyness and detachment to work with or talk to at least a few people. You will find that this skill, which you are developing tentatively now, will also be useful for you in the future.

I mentioned that the most well-functioning study groups are composed of friends who like and respect each other. But friendships within the field of economics can be difficult to manage. Let's face it: economics is not a discipline that encourages prosocial behavior. Individuals are considered chumps if they are too altruistic and not sufficiently self-seeking. This attitude tends to promote the development of self-interested individuals who don't know how to work with others even when it is in their interest to cooperate.

In the interest of providing economists with the full range of skills to optimize in all situations, herewith I provide some tips for how to behave in a study group.

1. Find a group that suits your study and social style.

- Some study groups like to meet frequently for long periods of time to solve problems together, as a group. Other groups prefer to meet briefly and less frequently, with most of the work done individually. It will drive you crazy if you are a once-a-week person but belong to a 24/7 group and vice versa. Find a group that satisfies your level of autonomy.

- Some groups comprise people who like to finish a problem set on Wednesday when it is due on Friday. Other groups like to stay up until 4:00 a.m. Friday to finish the same problem set. By now, you know the kind of person you are. Find others who work on the same schedule as you.

- How serious or hardcore a student are you? Are you satisfied with not always getting everything perfectly right? Or must you always push the limits of the problem, continually revising and refining your answers, adding more detail and depth to what the question asks? Do you feel it's important to set aside weekends to party and relax, or are you the type who studies every Saturday night? Both types are fine and exist in all graduate programs; you just need to find your tribe.

2. Don't be a user.

- Be a regular participant in the group, even when you don't want to and even when it's not always in your interest to do so. Don't come to group meetings only when you need help.
- Be generous with your knowledge. Help others who may not be as far along. Showing others how to solve problems or think about questions helps you clarify and solidify what you know and does a bit of good for your ego too.
- If you are too focused on getting your own needs met and are inconsiderate of others' needs, you will get a bad reputation (yes, even among self-interested economists) that will be hard to erase.

3. Pull your own weight. In other words, don't be a copycat.

- Do your own work. Make a good faith effort to complete all your own work and don't become too dependent on the study group to solve your problems.
- Study groups work because everyone makes a contribution, but if you are substantially weaker or less prepared than others in your study group, people will notice and become resentful. This is unfortunate, but it is human nature. If you find yourself in this position, you must redouble your efforts to catch up.
- Don't expect others to *always* help you; other people's generosity in helping you is a gift, not an entitlement. It may happen that you simply do not understand something or you are inadequately prepared to grasp what is required. Don't always push your study buddies to the edge by making them explain things to you until you understand it. Seek outside help, perhaps from your teaching assistant or a tutor, and work hard to compensate for your deficiencies.
- Being a copy-cat gives you a bad and long-lasting reputation for being both incompetent and unethical. Even though you

may view problem sets as a waste of time and thus no big deal to be cribbing the answers, the bad reputation you gain may extend into skepticism about the quality of your future research and your professional abilities.

4. A study group is not a cult or a life sentence.

- You can talk to other students about your problem sets. Although group members initially tend to be loyal to their own group, it is helpful socially and professionally to talk about problems with students outside your study group.
- If you are in a study group that is not ideal, don't be discouraged. Make the best of it. Find ways to learn what you need to learn, develop skills in being a leader and being a supportive group member, and make friends (or at least be collegial) with your study buddies.

So much for study groups, the first study strategy of graduate economics. The second study strategy is: track down old exams and problem sets and know how to solve the questions on them. In many departments, copies of previous years' qualifying exams and final course exams are publicly available. If this is not the case for your department, talk to students in previous years; they likely have a repository of old exams or at a minimum, copies of their own final course exams and qualifying exams. Students in these earlier cohorts have nothing to lose by giving these copies to you and are generally glad to help.

While you should aspire to learn the subject matter that you are taught rather than simply studying to the test, having old exams helps you prioritize your work. Even within a given subfield, so many papers and models are published that it is easy to get overwhelmed by the sheer quantity of material. The exams help you identify the important models, papers, and problem-solving techniques that keep coming up again and again. They help you separate the really important stuff (according to your department) from the less important things. Since you have limited time and energy, you want to focus your efforts on the really important topics. And knowing how to solve past problems gives you an idea of the range and types of problems you will be expected to solve.

Extracurricular Activities

Of course, first year is not *all* about coursework. There are the standard extracurricular activities with which you may be familiar from college: intramural sports, student government, community volunteering. There are also concerts, films, your favorite TV shows, jazz clubs, and house parties, not to mention girlfriends, boyfriends, spouses, and hook-ups.

Then there are the extracurricular activities that are unique to graduate school. These include the opportunity to be a teaching assistant or a research assistant for a professor. Or perhaps you are wondering whether you should start writing your own research papers, since this is the purpose of graduate school.

The time demands of the first year, especially if you are coming in without the advantages I noted earlier, are acute. But of course it is important to schedule leisure and activities having nothing at all to do with work. Supportive friendships and romantic relationships, and the social activities that enhance them, are certainly to be recommended.

As for the exact work-life balance, this is highly individual, but on this, I have two general guidelines. First, even though there is a fair amount of scheduling flexibility in graduate school, you should learn to treat grad school like a job. Try to set up a regular schedule: wake up at the same time very day, be consistent in the structure of your day or week in terms of work and leisure, work for X hours a day, and get to bed by a certain time each night. You don't have to wake up at 6:30 A.M.; your working day could be from noon to 4:00 A.M., but as long as it is consistent and works for you, this is what is important.

The second guideline is that it is neither optimal to work one day a week, nor is it optimal to work seven days a week. Based on my casual observation, moderately serious students work the equivalent of five to six full days per week. If you are coming in better prepared, you can get away with five days or possibly less; if you are less prepared, you may find some weeks where you will have to work seven full days a week, but this schedule is hard to sustain for an entire semester without losing your marbles. Unless you are coming to graduate school with a manservant, a housekeeper, or an incredibly accommodating partner, you will need to schedule time to do laundry, buy groceries, pay your bills, and take care of the chores of daily living.

As for whether to be a teaching assistant or a research assistant, there is general agreement that you absolutely should not be either a teaching assistant or a research assistant in your first year (alas, some departments require you to be a teaching assistant in your first year as a condition of the funding package—you're out of luck there). There will be plenty of time to be a teaching or research assistant in subsequent years when the opportunity cost is not as high in terms of taking away from your study time. If you really wish to be a research assistant (more on this later), you can always do this during summers when you have bigger blocks of time. So, as tempting as the offers may be, absolutely do not be a teaching assistant or a research assistant during your first year if you can at all avoid it.

As for doing your own research during your first year, this is always a good idea. Here, there is some disagreement on how much time you should spend on your research at the expense of your coursework. There are those who think that you should completely blow off your coursework and concentrate on your own research. After all, you are here to do independent research, and the earlier you start doing that, the better. Then there are those who think that you should build a good foundation and really master the coursework of the first (and second) year so that you can become a better researcher. Graduate school programs are designed so that you are given the foundational coursework first and then start working on research in your third year.

Ignoring your courses is a risky strategy. Unless you come into graduate school with the advantages that I mentioned earlier, it is unlikely that you have all of the technical skills that you need to be a professional Ph.D. economist. You won't know what the profession considers to be important questions to ask, nor whether the questions you pose have already been asked and answered. In addition, even though grades won't "count" on the job market (it's true, no one looks at your grad school grades), how professors in the department view you does matter. If you are producing B-level or C-level work, then even though faculty know that grades = effort + brains, they will usually assume you are incompetent, and this affects your reputation. Finally, some of the things that you learn in your courses may actually be helpful. If you blow off your courses, you will have a lot of gaps in your education that diminish your ability to be a good economist. Thus, the only way that this blowing-coursework-off strategy pays off is if you have already come in with a great deal of technical training and preparation. You know the material covered by coursework, so you won't do terribly in your classes. You already know the literature of the field in which you want to do research and you have the skills to do your own research. Very few students satisfy these criteria, but certainly some do.

Having said that, I am an advocate of spending at least some of your time (for example, ten hours a week) working on your own research during the first year. Doing this has a couple of advantages. First, it is good for your mental health. Many students feel frustrated spending so much of first year doing things that other people tell them to do. Working on your own ideas is a healthy and productive way to restore your own sense of autonomy. Second, thinking about concrete research projects will help you transform what you are learning into research ideas. This is a skill that will come in handy. Third, there is no substitute for the nuts and bolts of doing research. Even though coursework is important, solving problem sets is not a substitute for the practice of research. The earlier you start doing the practical work of research, the earlier you can make research mistakes (when they are not very costly) and the sooner you will find viable projects.

First-Year Exams

Departments vary in their attitude toward their Big Exams and when these exams occur. Some departments schedule Big Exams at the end of the first year. These exams, generally known as comprehensive exams, core exams, or preliminary exams, cover the content of the first-year courses. Other departments schedule their Big Exams at the end of the second year. These exams, known as field exams, general exams, or qualifying exams, are field specific, with the two fields chosen by the student. Some departments schedule Big Exams at the end of *both* the first year and the second year. And still other departments combine first-year final course exams with the Big Exams.

How high the stakes are with these Big Exams varies widely across departments. In many top departments, these Big Exams are not designed to fail or weed out students (the biggest weed-out already happened during the admissions process). In these departments, the exams are not particularly difficult or tricky, and almost everyone passes the first time; a few students each year are asked to do some remedial work or retake part of an exam in order to formally pass, but there is an understanding that this additional work is not too onerous, and that pretty much everyone will progress to the next stage.

In other departments, however, the first-year exams play a crucial role in screening or weeding out students. A nontrivial number of students fail some or all of the parts of the first-year exam and are given the opportunity to repeat the exam. If they fail a second time, they are not allowed to continue in the program. You will know if you are in one of these weeding-out programs (more on this in the "Weeding Out" section of this chapter).

Just as there is striking uniformity in the content of first-year courses, there is a great deal of uniformity in first-year exams. Many departments have exams in all three subjects—microeconomics, macroeconomics, and econometrics—while other departments test just on microeconomics and macroeconomics. Each exam on a subject can last up to two full days, so you can expect to take two to six days' worth of exams, spread out over several weeks.

If you have been doing well in your courses, there is no great art or strategy to studying for these comprehensive first-year exams. In most departments, each faculty member teaching a first-year course will be asked to contribute one or two questions to the exam. Thus, it is unlikely that you will be given a question that you have not seen in your courses, since the faculty who are writing the comprehensive exam are the same ones writing the final course exams.

So work through your old problem sets and previous years' problem sets and exams. There is usually a limited amount of time to study for these exams, so plan ahead to make sure that you are able to work through all of the material that you need to review in the allotted time. Study groups may or may not help. Stay away from stressed-out and stressful people and stressful situations. Of all the exams that you take in your graduate career, this may be one of the most important, so stay focused.

Finally, do not let up on nailing down the details. In many disciplines, comprehensive exams are a time when professors ask for overarching themes tying together disparate texts and literatures. In economics, there is a bit of that, but in the main, the level of detail that is expected for comprehensive exams is about the same as the level of detail that was expected for final course exams. Because exam time is limited, however, you will not be expected to do a very long derivation for a single question or model. For the (shorter) questions that you will be asked, you will still be expected to provide the same level of detail as in the problem sets or course exams.

Weeding Out

Although the practice of weeding out students during first year is no longer as common as it used to be, there are still some vestiges of it in some departments. In these departments, either the difficulty of their first-year courses induces students to drop out or the draconian first-year comprehensive exams tell students whether they made the cut or not. If you are in one of these programs, understand that it's not you, it's them. While there is nothing wrong with establishing standards and only wanting students who can clear the bar to progress in the program, departments that have this philosophy also have other features that make life difficult for students. For example, first-year courses are designed not so much to convey information as to identify the best students (i.e., the most prepared students, usually because of training received *before* entering the program). Faculty tend to not be so helpful and, in many cases, are not very interested in first-year students, since there is a positive probability that many of these students will not be around in subsequent years.

If you are in one of these programs, you will be in for a tough haul academically and emotionally the first year because of the generally poorer teaching and the lack of faculty support. Do what you need to do to find the intellectual and emotional support to survive in this difficult environment. In these kinds of departments, study groups and friendship groups are even more important. It would be a mistake to view your classmates as competitors; you are all in this together. Although there will always be some classmates who are overly competitive, find congenial ones who aren't. In addition, making friends outside the department will provide a good reality check. Get a tutor if you are having trouble academically; and find a counselor if you need to talk to someone who is not in the rat race.

Because of the psychological stress induced by the weeding-out system, students in these kinds of programs tend to have greater self-doubt than students in other programs—but this does not mean that they would make worse economists. Realize that the problem lies with the system and not necessarily with you.

A Few Final Words

So this is first year. You take courses, have a ton of challenges thrown at you, and are allowed to pass to the next level if you successfully tackle the challenges. Like boot camp, it will be difficult, but it will only last for a known and finite period of time. If you complete it, you will be stronger and more knowledgeable and ready to take on greater challenges. Having passed first year will be a real achievement, and you will, with good reason, be proud that you passed.

One way that graduate school is not like boot camp, however, is that military boot camp demands conformity. The most successful survivors of boot camp and perhaps the best military personnel are those who do whatever they are told by their commander. This is certainly not the case with graduate school. Although there is some uniformity in the material that you are presented, and you should master what is demanded of you, you should also take time to reflect on the material. Question it, understand its weaknesses, see how you can push it further. The best economists aren't the ones who just do what they are told and what others have done before them, but the ones who know the existing literature and choose to, in their own way, push its frontiers.

Notes

1. The secondary goal in some departments, especially those that have a reputation for weeding out students, is to identify the "best" students. More on this in the "Weeding Out" section of this chapter.

References

Mas-Colell, Andreu, Michael D. Whinston, and Jerry R. Green. 1995. *Microeconomic Theory.* New York: Oxford University Press.

Useful Web Pages

- econphd.net: http://econphd.econwiki.com/
- http://people.su.se/~mkuda/tips4economists.html

Chapter 4

Acing Second Year: Getting On with Graduate Life

Congratulations! You've passed the first year and made it to the second year of graduate school. It's all downhill (in a good way) from here. During the second year, you will have the opportunity to take courses in your specialized fields of interest, attend seminars, and start your own research projects. After the stresses of the first year, many students find the second year to be more relaxed and enjoyable, and relish the benefits of a more flexible schedule.

The greatest difficulty of the second year is that students stay too long in coursework mode and fail to make a productive transition to a research mindset. While the first-year courses were meant to be foundational, the second-year courses are meant to stimulate research ideas, so you should treat these courses differently from your first-year classes. In addition, you should begin to take advantage of the research environment offered by your department, such as seminars and workshops.

The Structure of the Second Year

The purpose of the second year is to transition you toward focused and productive research. To this end, students are offered courses that build upon the content and methods of the first year but are more focused. It is during this year that students choose the two fields in which they will specialize. Examples include behavioral economics, development economics, econometrics, financial economics, industrial organization, international economics, microeconomic theory, monetary theory, labor economics, and public economics. Students are often also required to take courses outside their two fields. Other required courses include an economic history course and a paper-writing course. They are also typically required to regularly attend a seminar series.

The second-year courses are structured differently from those of the first year. One might say that first-year courses are more like "greatest hits" courses, where students are presented with numerous classic models that "all economists must know." In the second-year courses, many models in a specific field are presented, but students are also expected to read the original papers, which often specify more complicated versions of the models. The treatment of the models and the papers is also very different. Whereas models in first year are presented as the research gold standard, models in the second year are presented with a critical eye, and students are expected to critique and improve upon them. They may also be expected to develop their own models, and some courses require independent research projects.

Students often fail to take full advantage of the project requirements that are part of their second-year courses. Part of this may be due to the fact that the project requirement is usually tacked onto the standard course requirements, and students are so busy studying for the course that they can only develop half-baked projects. But a second reason is that students are still in class-taking mode and have not quite switched to research mode, so they have not done the necessary thinking and work to develop a solid project. Make good use of these opportunities, especially if there are faculty and teaching assistants available who are, as part of this course, required to advise you on the project.

In most departments, there is also an expectation of a second-year paper. This is the student's first attempt at independent research.

It is often difficult to write a good second-year paper, both because of the time demands of coursework and preparing for exams and because it is hard to get everything right the first time around. Consequently, most second-year papers are really quite forgettable, but they are nevertheless good learning experiences. You get to know a literature well, and you see what it takes to push a project from the nub of an idea to a final paper. You find out what works and what doesn't, what the signals are of a dying project, what the big constraints are in a particular literature. The project and paper also give you the opportunity to develop relationships with certain faculty and check out their advising skills.

If you are fortunate, you will be able to eke out a paper that is publishable in a lower-tier journal. More likely, you will find that your project did not work out, but that you did develop an understanding, which you can further generalize, of why things did not turn out in the way you had hoped.

In addition to finishing up coursework requirements, second-year students are often required to attend seminars and workshops. Although departments differ in what they call a "seminar" as opposed to a "workshop" or "working group," I will use the term "seminar" to refer to a series in which outside speakers are invited to give a talk about their research. These speakers are often prominent faculty members from other institutions who present a well-developed or about-to-be published paper. Speakers are typically invited because someone in the department knows them or collaborates with them or is interested in their work. Sometimes they are invited because the faculty are interested in recruiting them to work for the department. Seminars are usually held weekly or, in smaller departments, biweekly or monthly.

In contrast to "seminars," I use the term "workshops" to refer to more informal presentations, mostly given by students but occasionally given by junior faculty. In these series, presentations are usually works in progress or projects in their early stages, and the participants are invited to offer suggestions.

Even though you are unlikely to understand much of the material that is presented, I would recommend that you be a regular attendee of at least one seminar series. You may also want to attend a workshop, although you may want to defer this to the third year, when you have papers of your own that you wish to present. Seminars are where a lot of intellectual activity takes place, and attending them is a good way to become socialized in the profession. In most economics seminars there is usually quite a bit of exchange between the speaker and the audience. Unlike in most other disciplines, the seminar is *not* a lecture in which the speaker goes on at length and then the audience politely asks questions at the end of the talk. Rather, the expectation is that audience members will ask questions and make comments throughout the talk, to clarify or to challenge or to make suggestions. Unlike in real life, it is not excessively rude to interrupt the speaker. Having said that, departments vary in their norms regarding the "correct" level of audience participation. You should carefully observe how the faculty behave, especially respected senior faculty, to learn what is "normal" or expected for the department.

Attending seminars where you have no idea what is going on most of the time will be difficult, but try to follow as much as you can. Treat a seminar like a class. Read or skim the paper ahead of time so that you know the broader and narrower purposes of the paper. Having read the paper, you will be much better able to follow the talk in real time. As you attend more and more seminars, you will begin to see patterns in the papers, and your research will benefit from seeing the broad range of papers produced by well-established faculty.

Doing Well in the Second Year

Unlike the first year, it is more difficult to determine who will do well in the second year. Certainly some students who do well in the coursework of the first year also do well in the coursework of the second year because of their preparedness. However, we often see students who were quite middling in their first year do very well in their second year. These students tend to be those who were not as well prepared but have managed to catch up and pick up the necessary technical skills for doing the work. In addition, it may be that studying a specialization in which they are interested motivates these students to put forth greater effort and do better.

The first-year course study strategies that I mentioned are just as applicable to the second year. Be careful of details and make good use of old problem sets and old exams. Study groups, though, play a less crucial role in the second year. One reason for this is that first-year study groups break up as students choose different fields in which to specialize, but another reason is that after the first year, students are generally on the same technical footing and there is not as great a need or use for group risk-sharing.

In addition to the basic study skills that were handy in the first year, you will want to develop the skills of critiquing papers, usefully modifying existing models, and developing your own models. More importantly, you will want to practice coming up with ideas that address the critiques you have of the existing literature. While first year was about learning the status quo, second year is about developing the skills to improve on the status quo.

Students who can add these new skills to their toolkit will do well in the second year. And as I have emphasized, those students who are able to successfully transition from classroom mode to research mode do the best. Some students who may not be as good in coursework, but have other skills or characteristics that are helpful for research, begin to emerge as serious students during this period. In particular, students who spend time reading and learning a specific literature, who have a critical eye that they can use to develop new projects, and who are self-starters will excel.

One thing that is nice about the second year is that faculty are more relaxed with second-year students and more accessible to them. If you are taking someone's field class, you are already interested in his or her area of research, and that can be a great basis for a relationship with a faculty member. Take the time to talk to your professor about the literature, about research that she or he is working on, and about your own ideas. Taking his or her course is an excellent low-key way to get to know faculty members.

Studying for Second-Year Exams

For students in programs that have first-year exams, second-year field exams will appear to be much, much easier. They certainly will be far less stressful. You passed the first-year exams, so you know what to expect in terms of technical proficiency, and you know what you need to do to prepare for these kinds of exams. Here, students stumble when they are lulled into complacency by the relaxed attitude of the professors and the lower intensity of the courses. Students do poorly when they simply don't put in the hours and time to prepare for the exams. This is a foolish and completely avoidable mistake to make. Even if you have been blowing off your courses, take the weeks prior to the field exams to focus and prepare for them. After all, they will be the very last exams you will ever have to take.

For students in programs that only have second-year exams, the pressure can be a bit more intense. Certainly, you don't have the experience of the first-year exams to reassure yourself that you know how to prepare for them. And these exams will not be easy or pro forma in the way that they are in programs that give first-year exams. On the whole though, especially if you are in a top-ranked department, everyone is expected to pass, even if a few people have to retake parts of an exam or do additional work to earn a pass.

If you are taking the Big Exam for the first time, adopt the disciplined attitude that I recommended for those taking first-year comprehensive exams. Use course material and reading-list material to prepare for the exams seriously. Plan a schedule so that you will be able to cover all of the topics that you are required to know before the exam date hits. Review old problem sets and previous years' problem sets and exams. Then review them in detail again and know how to answer the problems cold.

Extracurricular Activities

Since the second-year course load will be (or seem) lighter than the first-year load, you may be tempted to reward yourself by doing all of those things that you put off doing last year. Although you can certainly afford the time to participate in *a few* more activities that you enjoy, you should restrain yourself from attempting to do too many of them. Sure, increase your leisure time, but don't commit yourself to activities that give you no flexibility in the amount of time you devote to them. You are in graduate school to learn how to do research and this should be your first priority, so don't get distracted with metastasizing long-term commitments to student government or being graduate resident head (unless you see that as part of your long-term professional goal); leave that until later, or to other students who plan on staying in grad school longer than you.

And the advice that I gave regarding TAing and RAing still stands. To the extent that you have additional time, spend that time developing your own research projects or attending seminars and workshops. Use the courses and others' research as a jumping-off point for your own work. And enjoy the beginning of your independent intellectual life.

Chapter 5

Finding a Topic and an Advisor: Like Getting Married . . . to a Polygamist

The worst is over. You are done with all the courses that you will ever have to take in your entire life. You are a free person.

But like most newly released prisoners, you will need to adjust to your new life and its freedoms. Some people adjust well, others badly. I'm here to orient you to this new world and to help you make the adjustment in the best way you can.

A Flyover of the Rest of Your Graduate Years

Now that we've dispensed with the first two years, here is a flyover of the rest of graduate school. Unlike the first two years of your graduate program, the rest of your program can be as long or as short as you want to make it. After your coursework years, you will be given a period of time—typically a year—in which you will be expected to develop an idea for a dissertation; this dissertation, depending on the department, will be either a single über-paper or a series of three papers. You will be asked to write up the dissertation idea in what is called a prospectus or proposal, which a committee consisting of 2-4 faculty members (whom you have selected) must approve. In some departments, there is an oral exam in which you are required to defend your prospectus.

After your committee has approved your prospectus, you are considered to have advanced to candidacy (so you can now be called a Ph.D. candidate) and you will have as many years as you can afford to complete your research. During this candidacy period, you may be asked to be a teaching assistant or a research assistant.

When you have tired of graduate school or have run out of money, you put together a paper that has some hope of being published or at least of not being laughed at, and you go on the job market. If all goes well, you go to interviews at the American Economic Association (AEA) meetings in January, get invited for flyouts to various prospective employers, are presented with multiple job offers, and accept one of these. Almost as an afterthought, you must "defend" your dissertation in what is typically a brief oral presentation of your work, whereupon, after wearing a gown with suitable gravitas, you are conferred a Ph.D. degree.

This sounds complicated, but it really isn't. Luckily, the faculty and department administrators have had many years of experience shepherding confused students through this process. You can usually trust that the administrators will tell you what you need to do and when to do it and whose signatures you need. You can also rely on students farther along in the program to help you through the process.

So those are the mechanics. What about the big picture? Well, remember the gulf between undergraduate and graduate economics? Multiply that by 10,000. The third year and subsequent years are nothing like the two years of coursework that preceded them.

The purpose of the coursework years was to give you the technical foundation to do research. The purpose of the post-coursework years is to give you the time and freedom to do said research. More accurately, it gives you the time to take a first crack at doing research, and it gives you people who have the power to tell you when you are done messing around. That is all. We may hope that we get kind mentors, gentle guidance, and good advice along the way, but nowhere in any graduate program handbook have I seen this in writing. Mostly, you are on your own. Which, to be honest, is how you will be when you are a professor doing independent research.

On good days, you may get helpful advice. But the bulk of your success and productivity in the rest of your graduate years is up to you. This is both exciting and frightening. I hope to give you enough information so that you will find this prospect more exciting than frightening.

Doing Well in the Third Year and Subsequent Years

Empirically, although there is a positive correlation between students who do well in their coursework and those who go on to be successful in the job market and in research, it is frequently the case that many students who do well in their coursework do not do as well in later years. Conversely, some students who were pretty mediocre in class do extremely well in the research years. We don't know all the reasons for this, but I can highlight a few characteristics of students who do well in the research part of graduate school:

1. *They have a good work ethic.* They put in the hours. They focus on their research, whether it's reading the literature, writing code, or working through the math.
2. *They are independent self-starters.* They do not need faculty to constantly guide them and reassure them. If they find they need something—an old paper, a skill, a dataset—they go out and get it. They do not need faculty to push them along or check up on them.
3. *They have ideas.* They have a large stock of research ideas or know how to generate them. They do not need faculty to give them research ideas.

These characteristics are by no means sufficient characteristics. One can think of other traits that are important—creativity, organizational skills, communication skills—but the ones I emphasized are surely necessary. If you don't have them, you are unlikely to finish the graduate program, much less do well. Of course, having these qualities does not guarantee that you will get a good job—you can work hard to write a careful job market paper based on a dumb idea—but it does guarantee that you will come up with *something*, which is more than many graduate students are able to achieve.

Some people, either through their life experience or through training, seem to have these characteristics in spades. Others appear to be more challenged. If you are someone for whom these things do not come naturally, try to develop them as part of your professional skill set, like solving Hamiltonians or public speaking. They may never come naturally, but you can always develop them further.

If you find yourself a bit undisciplined, develop little tricks to force yourself to work. Set a timer for 45-minute intervals and tell yourself that you have to work until the timer goes off; reward yourself a bit when you are done. Disable your browser, log off your e-mail, and turn off your cell phone. Also, remind yourself that there was a period of time when you were able to work hard. Remember trying to solve a difficult problem or studying for your exams? Or what about getting to the next level of Halo, or doing research on power rankings so that you could fill out your NCAA bracket? You have shown that you have the ability to focus and to work. Find that again within yourself. Read a self-help book, take a personal development course, or talk to a life coach or counselor. They all have good ideas about how you can better develop focus and discipline.

What if you are not a self-starter? What if you really do need others to motivate you or show you how to do things? While we can't be completely self-sufficient, we can all be less dependent along some dimension than we currently are. For example, when you were applying to graduate schools, presumably you didn't have your mother tell you where to apply, send you the links to the application form, and complete the form for you (did you?). You developed a list of graduate programs to which to apply—based perhaps on the recommendation of faculty members, or on the rankings of *U.S. News & World Report*, or on discussions about school reputations among your classmates—and you went online to find the application websites. Similarly, break down your research needs into small, self-contained tasks and complete them. Go online or read papers to get ideas on how others have handled similar problems. Just start *doing* and more leads will come.

Having trouble with generating research ideas? I suspect there are two main reasons some students have a hard time with ideas. The first is that they don't have enough raw material. That is, they don't read enough or don't question what they read enough, or they fail to connect what they read and hear with potential research projects. All of these problems can be practically remedied: read more (either popular writing or academic papers, or ideally both); start looking for things that you don't like in a paper and think about what you would have done instead; and when you hear a news story or a fact, ask yourself the question, how could I study this or how could this be turned into a research project?

The second reason students think they have no ideas is really, they actually *do* have ideas but they quickly rule them out as being too dumb. Now it's entirely true that you and I and everybody else can generate bad ideas. But at this stage, the usual problem is being too critical too early, not the other way around. Especially in top programs, where there is an inordinate amount of emphasis on having The Blockbuster Idea, students (and faculty too, by the way) are too critical too early of others' ideas and of their own. Start small, with something less ambitious, so that you can see how this research business works, then aim higher. What contributes to the problem is that it is possible to talk too soon about your ideas. In this profession, we are trained to be acutely critical, so our first instinct is to find everything that is wrong or that might not work. If this criticism comes at too early a stage, plenty of good, potentially publishable papers get scrapped, and you wind up discouraged and idea-less. If you are one of these people who think they have no ideas, consider working on your silly proto-ideas for a while, and seeing if they will work, before you start talking to others.

I started off this section talking about the characteristics of students who do well in their post-coursework years. You may have noticed that much of the discussion that followed was really about the psychology of managing your research years. Now, as economists, who put a great deal of stock in people's *behaviors* and not so much in pretending to know what goes on inside people's heads, we may be tempted to dismiss this advice as squishy mumbo jumbo. But the main point that you should take away about this period in your life is that the hard part here is not managing your intellectual life; it is managing your emotional and psychological life. This much is clear: by the time you've passed your courses and your qualifying exams, we know that you have the technical skills and the intellect to do good economic research. Thus, what distinguishes the people who pass through this next phase from those who are spat out by it is their resilience.

In addition to encouraging you to develop these psychological skills, which you may never have had to develop, I have three more practical suggestions. First, stop taking courses. For some of you, this may be a no-brainer; why take more courses than the absolute minimum you are required to take? For others, some of who may have insecurities about not knowing enough, there is the temptation to continually take courses to fill in all of the perceived gaps in your training. But taking classes takes away time, and although you may think that after the required coursework you've got all the time in the world, research also takes a great deal of time. And in research there are often increasing returns, so you won't be nearly as productive in research as you think you will be if you are spending a lot of time in classes.

Certainly it's fine to audit a course here and there. But the only good reason for auditing a class is if it covers a problem that you are currently tackling. Even then, though, you may not have to take the entire course and can just sit in on the lectures that cover material directly related to your research. Occasionally, you may want to attend a few lectures given by a resident or visiting faculty member who has an amazing reputation but who rarely teaches or who has an idiosyncratic approach to some literature related to your work. This is not a bad idea. But the reasons I've spelled out are really the only reasons you should be auditing a course. Do not take a course because you think you might need it in the future or you want to see what it's about. These are all fine and good intellectual reasons, of course, but time is limited and if you do find you need these methods or this subject later, you can learn them then, instead of as part of some global ignorance-reducing strategy.

In the discussion of the second year, I recommended attending a seminar series regularly. You should keep attending seminars, but in third and subsequent years, the problem may lie in wanting to attend too many seminars. At a research university, there are usually lots of interesting talks going on, but you really should restrain yourself from spending your time listening to others' research at the expense of doing your own. I would recommend going to at least one seminar a week but not more than two. And while you may be tempted to cherry-pick talks within a seminar series to go to, I would recommend being a regular attendee of one series in your field of interest. This way, you get to know the broad range of research going on within your field, and in addition, everyone appreciates a team player they can count on to show up. For the other series, it's fine to show up occasionally for those talks that are of most interest to you.

Beginning in the third year, you should also try to be a regular participant in a working group. As I mentioned earlier, working groups consist of graduate students who present their work in progress. Some departments formally set up topic-centered working groups so that faculty members can attend and give advice. In other departments, you may have to form your own working group. If this is the case, choose four or five students who are working in the same subfield and, ideally, whom you find helpful in discussing ideas. It is often useful to have a faculty member or two attend the working group, since their attendance generally prevents the discussions from degenerating into social talk and also motivates students to show up regularly. Working groups should be a low-risk environment, so students feel free to present half-baked ideas and early attempts, and audience members should try to be constructive and encouraging.

Try to present your work at least once a year, and ideally, much more frequently. In student-run working groups where there are only four or five of you, you could present as frequently as once a month. This will give you practice in orally presenting your research and in fielding questions (you don't want your job talk to be the first time you are presenting your research!). You will also get feedback from a broader audience than if you were to just speak one-on-one to friends or faculty.

Lastly, in this research period, you should make it a priority to learn to be a professional. By this I mean, treat the post-coursework period as if you were already in a job—let's call you a pre-professor. Professors are expected to show up on time to teach their classes, attend seminars, show up to meetings, work seriously on their research, be good colleagues. Pre-professors should similarly show up on time to TA their classes, attend seminars, show up to meetings they set up with faculty and working groups, work seriously on their research, be good colleagues. As I recommended in the previous chapter, set up a regular work schedule, but also learn to be a dependable, helpful, and professional colleague. In short, get your act together.

Now, maybe you have already decided that you don't want to be a professor or even a pre-professor. Fair enough. I discuss this possibility in the next chapter. But for the rest of you, if you aspire to be a professor, start acting like one.

Finding the Right Topic

The title of this section is a bit misleading. It assumes that there is such a thing as the *right* topic. The reality is that there is no single right topic or even multiple right topics, but there are many good and sensible ones for you.

There is an attitude, either explicit or implicit, in many departments that the third and subsequent years should be spent finding your Blockbuster Job Market Paper. It goes without saying that this expectation puts tremendous pressure on students, and this attitude is responsible for the creative constipation that many students experience.

Of course, it is an empirical regularity that working on an ill-conceived bad paper takes as much if not more time and effort than working on a good paper. So, given a limited amount of time, you are much better off working on a really good idea. Having said that, working on a bad idea strictly dominates chasing the mythical Blockbuster Paper, never quite finding it, and ending up with a poorly developed idea and a shoddy paper. The problem is that students waste inordinate amounts of time trying to come up with The Big Idea that will get them a tenure-track job at Prestigious U. Instead of working on *something*, they run hither and yon and find themselves at the end of their fourth year with no viable ideas, and have to rush to put together a slap-dash paper so that they can go on the market before their funding runs out. This is a terrible way to end graduate school but it happens to many students.

One underappreciated fact is that, in research, there is a lot of learning to be gained by the actual *doing* of research, even bad research. And yes, your first few ideas and papers will be bad. Or what I really mean is, they will be worse than the ones you come up with later. So get the bad stuff out of the way by starting to work sooner rather than later.

In concrete terms, what does this mean? It means, first of all, you should set yourself a deadline for committing to your first real research project. I would recommend using your second-year paper requirement or one of your research-oriented second-year course requirements for this first project. Commit to working on this project from start to finish so that you see what it takes to write a serious paper. Likely you will find that your research or proof strategy didn't work, things got more complicated than you had anticipated, you couldn't get the data you wanted, and the data that you were able to get were terrible. Welcome to the real world of research. If the paper has any remotely new result and is publishable, albeit in a bottom-ranked journal, you should send it in and have the experience of going through the process of peer review. If you essentially had to abort the project because the statement you wanted to prove was actually false or because you couldn't get the data to do the project, you should file the project away and consider it a useful learning experience. This was your freebie.

While you are working on this maiden project, you should be

thinking of other project ideas. When the first project is done, you will then have a list of possible ideas. Choose several of the more promising ones and start working on these. But set a deadline for yourself a month down the road to reassess how promising the various projects are. Also, continue to generate new ideas even while you are working on these projects. At the end of the month, assess where you are, drop the less promising ones, continue the promising ones, and start working on new ones to replace the projects you dropped.

A new development in economics is the emergence of large (multi-person) long-term projects. As a graduate student, you may be considered prime labor input for these large experimental or "big data" empirical projects. Although these projects can be great learning experiences, they can also be risky. Students may have to invest a great deal of time learning large swaths of literature outside of economics (e.g., neuroscience, psychology). They may find themselves stuck having to do essentially administrative work (e.g., putting together paperwork for the Institutional Review Board, making phone calls) for quite uncertain payoffs. Since these projects can take many years to prepare, the results from these studies may not be ready for analysis by the time you are on the job market and need a paper. Put differently, the project may well continue but you will not be the beneficiary of it. Or you may find that the data quality or findings are worse than expected because of unanticipated bureaucratic difficulties. Or the findings may be quite good but with so many people involved in the project, more senior investigators may take credit for the work and your prior contribution will be minimized.

Having said that, if this is the kind of economics that you wish to pursue as an independent researcher, it is in your interest to become involved in these projects as a graduate student. You will learn a broad range of skills—analytical, technical, managerial, administrative, political—that are required to successfully run these kinds of projects and that will serve you well after you graduate. At the same time, you should make sure that you will leave the Ph.D. program with evidence of (i.e., papers that demonstrate) your ability to do economic research.

Toward that end, here are two pieces of advice. First, become involved in multiple projects that are in different stages of development. Ideally, you want to become involved in at least one project from its inception so you can get in at the ground level; it is best to join these in your first or second year of graduate school or possibly earlier. You should know, however, that there is a risk that the project won't be completed by the time you are on the market. For this reason, you will want to become a part of other projects that are farther along, so you will have something to show for your efforts.

Second, carve out a part of each project that is unambiguously your own. Come to an agreement with the principal investigator that a certain part of the experiment (or data or project) will be considered yours, where you will be the lead author. Put this in writing and be clear that everyone understands this. In this way, you will have some tangible evidence of the effort you put into this multi-person project.

Regardless of whether you are a lone theorist, a data junkie, or a group experimentalist, by the end of your third year, you should have a portfolio of ideas that you have tried out and that look like they will work. From among these, choose two or three of your best ideas and focus your energy on these. Ideally, they will all be on the same or related topics, but it is not a big deal if they are not. These will be the projects on which you will base your proposal.

Finding the Right Advisors

Students agonize over choosing the right advisor. As with topics, there are no right advisors, only advisors who are better or worse for you. Sad to say, you may find that in all but the biggest departments, you will not have much of a choice with advisors. This is because departments have, at most, three or four individuals working in a given subfield. In many cases, even they will not know much about your specific topic, but they do know about related literatures or the subfield as a whole, and they will be able to serve as advisors.

For your chair, you should choose someone who is senior and who likes you or likes your projects. This person will be very important for your candidacy going smoothly and for your job market experience, so it is crucial that he likes you or, failing that, likes your work (or at a minimum, doesn't think it is ill-conceived or pointless). This person should be senior and tenured (read, experienced) because you want someone who is well respected, who has lots of friends in the profession, and who understands how the system works.

Aside from the obvious heavy hitters, whether someone is well respected and has friends can be hard to discern from where you are sitting. Clearly, your own department likes him and respects him—after all, they hired him and gave him a tenured position—but this may not be a good signal of how he is viewed in the profession at large. He could be an oddball or a loose cannon who hasn't built up a lot of stock among his peers. Note that this is not the same as saying that he is devoid of social skills. Frequently, many professors who seem socially awkward to you are respected and liked in the profession, so don't base your judgments on how strange or eccentric people appear to be.

Many graduate students are intimidated by senior faculty and tend to have closer relationships with junior faculty. This is natural and to be expected, but this doesn't mean these junior faculty should chair your committee. They should certainly be on your committee, since they are the ones who are most likely to give detailed practical advice that you might actually find useful, but they will mostly be considered unknown quantities in the profession so they should not play the lead role. It would be great if the chair knew your projects well and read your papers and gave you detailed suggestions, but surprisingly, this is not necessary. Many times, the chair is more of a big-picture strategy person. The kind of advice that she gives relates to whether there is a market for your paper, how you should position a paper within the literature, how it is likely to be received, and relatedly, the broad critiques that it might face.

As for the other committee members, you should again include people who like you and like your projects. These members should be people who have particular expertise in the topic or the methods used in your papers, and at least one of them should be the kind of person who will read your paper thoroughly and give you detailed comments and suggestions.

Students are often tempted to choose advisors who are super famous. While a faculty member being super famous is not a bad thing, bear in mind that his reputation is based on his research output, not on his ability to inject his genius into his students, his advising skills, or his ability to place his students in good jobs. Nor is it based on his charming personality. In general, regardless of how prominent someone is, you want to avoid crazy or difficult advisors. You don't need that stress in your life, and students often find, ruefully, that the payoff they had expected for putting up with their advisor's craziness never comes, because—guess what?—the person was crazy and unpredictable to begin with.

Along with the benefits of having a good committee and set of advisors comes the responsibility of being a good advisee. I caution that this does not come naturally, partly because this will be your first (and only) time being an advisee, and most students come in with unrealistic expectations.

Even the best, most kindly advisors have lives of their own. Not to sound snotty, but faculty, especially the senior faculty, have lives that are far busier than yours. Let me put this differently. In addition to doing the research that you have to do (multiplied by ten), they have to teach, serve on university committees, serve on professional boards and associations, referee and edit journal articles, review funding proposals, organize and present at conferences and seminars, act as consultants, attend social activities for visiting faculty and job candidates, and deal with the university administration and the media. They may also have families and ex-wives and stepchildren. Moreover, whereas you have one chair and one committee, they have multiple students to advise in different capacities, including possibly undergraduates, and multiple dissertation committees of which they are a part. So while you are monogamously married to your advisor and your own projects, she is rather polygamously married to many students and many commitments. As part of her job and her sense of duty, she has agreed to be one of your advisors. She has limited time but of the time she has, some of it is earmarked for you. So, use your time with your advisor wisely. Go to the appointments you set up with her, be on time, be prepared, teach yourself what you need to know, and do the work you said you would do. Bear in mind that in practical terms she gets very little in return from advising you except the satisfaction of helping a student pass through the gauntlet.

It is also important to emphasize that your advisor is not your mother (or father), your therapist, or your best friend. You are in a work relationship with this person: act professionally. She may of course be quite friendly and take you out for coffee and ask after your family and your well-being, and that is fine, but this just means she's a human being. At the end of the day, your relationship with her is first and foremost a professional (i.e., work) one; there is a power differential between the two of you—at least while you are a graduate student and she is a faculty member—regardless of how personally compatible you are, so you must act accordingly. This doesn't mean that you should act like a detached automaton and only talk about research, but it does mean you shouldn't over-share about your personal and emotional life, complain about other faculty, or gossip about other students or faculty. Some professors are used to being therapists for their students and are fine with this being part of their job description, but don't bet on it.

Your advisors are there to help you with your research, but ultimately you are responsible for your own education and the management of your own life. If you stay realistic about what your advisors can and cannot do for you, you can make the most of this relationship.

Preparing for the Oral Exam on Your Prospectus

Oral exams on your prospectus vary in style across different departments, but they follow a similar structure. You will need to schedule a block of time (usually one to two hours) during which all your committee members can be present. Several weeks prior to the exam, you need to submit a proposal or prospectus detailing your proposed research projects. Although you are ostensibly "propos-ing" to do something, it is likely that you have already done some of the work for one or two research projects. This prospectus docu-ment will be circulated among the faculty.

At the hearing, you start by giving a presentation of your re-search projects. Expect to be interrupted shortly into your presenta-tion. You will be asked questions of all kinds: Why did you choose this research question? Why are you answering the question in this way? Isn't this alternative method a better way? What do you think of this literature or a related literature (or occasionally, because it is someone's pet topic, a completely unrelated literature)? How does your research fit into the literature? What do you think of X paper? Why did you not cite Y paper? Have you considered doing Z?

Expect to be asked questions that you have clearly answered in your prospectus document because the faculty may not have read it or won't remember it even if they had read it. Anticipate the possi-bility that a faculty member may tell you to do the complete opposite of what she told you to do six months ago, or the complete opposite of what another committee member told you to do. Expect that they might be disappointed or extremely critical of your projects because what you are doing is very different from what they thought you were doing.

Depending on the personalities of the faculty members and whether the department views the oral exam as a screening process or pro forma exercise, you may be faced with either hostile questions or constructive suggestions. Bear in mind, though, that your chair would not have let you schedule the exam unless she felt that you were ready, and that the committee was ready to approve your pro-spectus. Thus, unless the chair is terribly careless in keeping up with what you've been up to, there should be no surprises in terms of the committee approving your prospectus.

How should you prepare for such an exam? First of all, be reas-sured that you know more than you think you do about your project. After all, you have been working on this project in far greater depth than any of your committee members, so you know the literature and the research better than they do.

You will want to brainstorm all the possible questions that they can ask you. This may be a long list. Focus particularly on the literature leading up to your paper, the biggest challenges of your research projects, and how you have dealt with or propose to deal with these challenges. Since you are being examined on a *proposal*, if you don't know how to deal with a problem, it is quite okay to say that you've thought about this problem, have a few ideas, but would appreciate any suggestions that the committee would have to offer.

Although your prospectus will most likely be approved, the exam can go badly if you cannot justify why you have chosen a particular research strategy over another (and are not open to modifying the strategy), if you appear not to have understood or thought through your research problem, or if there is a fatal flaw in your project. You want to show that, even though you may not know everything that the committee asks you, at least you've been thoughtful about your research.

Your Job as Joe or Jill Candidate

Many faculty members look back on graduate school and view the post-coursework years as the happiest years of their research lives. You have few demands on your time and little immediate pressure to produce. It is tempting to spend this time engaging in TV-watching marathons, documenting all your activities on Facebook, or going on an extended world tour. Until an administrative deadline approaches, no one is going to check up on whether you've even been in your cubicle the last six months.

But bear in mind that you will never again have this amount of free research time, even after tenure, and you will certainly not have the same kind of entitled access to very smart people who are obliged to give you advice. Treat this time preciously. I have been advocating that you treat your third year and beyond as your pre-professor job, but a job need not mean drudgery. When you graduate, if you stay in academia, you will have one of the most liberating and envied jobs in the world. Consider yourself lucky that you can have a pre-professor job that is even better than that dream job you are going to get. Make the most of it.

Further Reading

Creedy, John. 2001. "Starting Research." *Australian Economic Review* 34: 116–124.

Creedy, John. 2007. "A Ph.D. Thesis Without Tears." University of Melbourne Department of Economics Research Paper No. 987.

Hamermesh, Daniel. 1992. "The Young Economist's Guide to Professional Etiquette." *Journal of Economic Perspectives* 6: 169–179.

Hamermesh, Daniel. 2005. "An Old Male Economist's Advice to Young Female Economists." *CSWEP Newsletter* Winter 2005: 11–12.

Szenberg, Michael, ed. 2008. *Passion and Craft: How Economists Work*. Ann Arbor: University of Michigan Press.

Thomson, William. 1999. "The Young Person's Guide to Writing Economic Theory." *Journal of Economic Literature* 37: 157–183.

Thomson, William. 2001. *A Guide for the Young Economist*. Cambridge, Mass.: MIT Press.

Chapter 6

Getting Distracted: TAing, RAing, and the Meaning of Life

I've spent the last several chapters talking about the academic part of graduate school. But there is a large part of grad school that does not relate to academia at all. In this chapter, I discuss a hodgepodge of issues that frequently arise during graduate school but are not really at the core of the academic experience. If you handle them well, they will enhance your grad school experience; if they go wrong, they will create completely unnecessary stress that can hurt your academic performance.

Being a Teaching Assistant

A staple of the graduate school experience is being a teaching assistant (TA). As a TA, you will be expected to run discussion sections, give supplemental lectures, grade problem sets and exams, hold office hours to answer students' questions, and generally assist the professor in running the course, doing whatever it is that she does not want to do. You may be asked to TA for either undergraduate classes or graduate classes.

Teaching assistantships pay a nominal amount and are typically a required part of the graduate funding package. While the department often frames TAing as a pedagogical experience for you, it really isn't; it's cheap labor for the department. This doesn't mean that you can't learn something from the TA experience, but it does mean that you should be wary of such "opportunities."

If you are primarily interested in a research career, even if you love teaching and care deeply about students—something for which you should be commended by the way—it is in your interest to minimize the amount of TAing that you do. I'm not being a jerk; I'm being realistic. If you are required to TA, you should do it, obviously, but if there is no TAing requirement and you're doing it for the money, see if you can't cut your budget or take out loans. (There are some exceptions to this advice—see below.)

The biggest difficulty with being a TA is that it is unambiguously a time sink that redirects your efforts away from research, which unfortunately is the only thing that counts when you start applying for academic jobs. Yes, you may gain experience in standing up and speaking in front of people, but it's entirely possible to get more relevant experience by participating in seminars and working groups.

But, you may say, since you will have to teach your own courses as a research professor, might it not be a good idea to TA first? As it happens, there is not that close a relationship between what you do as a TA and your future teaching as a professor, so the gains would be small. In fact, preparing to give a job market talk, one that is carefully laid out and speaks to a broad audience, probably provides better experience for teaching than TAing (and is in fact what employers use to evaluate your teaching ability). As a concession, though, I would say that it might be useful to TA perhaps one or two courses in your graduate career to get a sense of the teaching experience and to learn how to deal with students.

There are two exceptions to this TAing advice. First, if you truly love teaching and look forward to a career that is teaching-intensive or that is more balanced in terms of teaching and research, then you should take advantage of the teaching opportunities that your department offers. You should bear in mind, however, that at many top liberal arts colleges, there is still an expectation of research (although greater flexibility in the type of research and frequency of publication), so you still need to balance your teaching and research commitments. If this is the path for you, try to TA a broad range of courses so that you can develop a variety of pedagogical skills, and get a sense of what you'd like to teach and how you would like to teach it. At some point, probably after two or three semesters of TAing, you should try to teach your own course. This gives you excellent experience in developing your own material and is a good way to show prospective employers that you are serious about teaching and have the skills they want. You should try to teach two of your own courses, one of which is a staple course (e.g., Intermediate Microeconomics) and another elective course that reflects your subject interest (e.g., Environmental Economics). Many departments have teaching shortages, especially with their undergraduate courses, so they would be more than happy to give you a lecturing slot if you showed an interest. In addition, there may be community colleges in the area that are looking for adjunct lecturers and willing to give you an opportunity to run your own course.

A second exception is if you happen to be in a lower-ranked department (ranked 50 or below). As a practical matter, when you graduate, your academic job opportunities may lie more in teaching-oriented institutions rather than research institutions. If this is the case, it may be helpful to take advantage of TAing opportunities in your department. I would, however, also recommend seeking opportunities to teach your own courses since you will get more relevant experience this way.

As a last word on TAing and teaching, even though it is indeed a time sink, once you have agreed to be TA for a course, you should do your best to be a competent TA. Prepare for your discussion sections, be at office hours when you say you will be, be as helpful as you can to your students. We have undoubtedly all been on the other side, bemoaning lazy TAs who have failed to do their work and have been unwilling to help us, so give a little back and make an effort to do your job well.

Being a Research Assistant

An option that many students have, especially those working in empirical fields, is to be a research assistant (RA). As an RA, you may be asked to do literature reviews, look for data sets, clean up data, do statistical programming and analysis, derive or generalize a result, and perhaps edit a bit. There are two lines of thought on whether you should be an RA in graduate school. The first is that you should never ever RA for anyone at any point during graduate school (it is, however, still a good idea to RA *prior* to grad school). The reason given is that grad school should be about doing your own research, and you should be investing your time in your own projects instead of being a grunt for someone else.

The second line of thought is that it is not a bad idea to RA in the early years of graduate school because you can learn quite a lot about research that you can't learn anywhere else, or that you will eventually have to find out in more costly ways on your own. It is helpful to see how a good project is conducted and how an experienced researcher handles frustrations and details such as manuscript revision. And if there is potential for you to be a coauthor, then you may have an opportunity to be published in a higher-quality journal than you would otherwise be able to get into on your own.

My view is that there is a finite benefit to being an RA, but the best time to RA is before you go to graduate school. If you did not RA before grad school and feel you need the experience now before starting your own projects, being an RA for ten to fifteen hours a week, or for a summer, is not a bad idea. There are, however, additional conditions. First, you must make sure that your professor is not a crazy or overly demanding person. Graduate school is challenging enough without the additional stress of managing your professor and the demands of the RA work. Second, there should be a good chance that you will be a coauthor. Before you start, you should be clear on the amount and type of work that is required to be granted coauthorship. If coauthorship is not likely, you will have to think much harder about whether the other benefits are sufficient (e.g., developing particular research skills, working with a smart and likable person who has interest in mentoring you, getting access to data). Third, make certain the project is advanced enough so that it has a high likelihood of being published. You would be surprised at how many projects disappear into black holes, even after great investments of time, energy, and RAs. Becoming involved early in a project has risks for you as a graduate student, so you are better off signing onto a project where there is already a clear view of the final product being published. Finally, I emphasize, only get involved if you truly have no experience in this area of research but would like to pursue research projects on your own in this field. You will get the most intellectual and professional benefit this way.

Friends, Lovers, and Families

Among the happiest students in graduate school are those who feel a part of their cohort and graduate program, who have friends in the program and outside it, and who have an intimate romantic partner (girlfriend/boyfriend/spouse). It helps of course if they feel they are making good progress on their research, but really the social connections are what helps students feel generally happy with their day-to-day grad school life.

This means that you should take care of these relationships. While it is tempting to view classmates as rivals, in the long run most if not all of your classmates are unlikely to work in exactly the same research area as you (and hence will not be competing with you). It just makes more sense to foster a relationship of friendship with your classmates, rather than rivalry. Since it is more difficult to develop friendships once you are working as an assistant professor, most friendships within the profession in fact start off as friendships going back to grad school.

Economists are not particularly known for their social skills, so this is an area in which it is always useful to make an investment. This helps you both in the present and in the future. Studies in the psychology literature have shown that students don't need a boatload of friends, just one good friend, to not feel socially isolated. These students enjoy their time in school more, so having friends helps you today. But with friendships, you are also investing in the future. Because you are all going to be economists, you are more than likely going to see these friends and acquaintances in the future in a professional context. Of course, you should not view people merely as professional bank accounts, so the main point here is, be careful of burning bridges over petty disagreements in grad school. I might also mention that, with the high-pressure environment of economics graduate programs, it might be helpful to make friends who are not in the economics program or who are not in school at all. They can give you a reality check on some of the dramas of grad school life.

In addition to friendships, it is a good idea to take care of your romantic relationships. Many marriages and dating relationships break up in grad school, especially during the first year of the program. Of course, these relationships might have broken up anyway, but my guess is that, with the demands of school, it is very easy to become self-absorbed and selfish. Partners dislike this kind of thing. It is possible to survive graduate school with your relationship intact if you prepare your partner for the pressure you will be facing. But it is important that you make a distinction between being very busy and being a selfish jerk. Partners in the real world want to be supportive and accommodating, but they are not saints. Set aside the time and energy to sustain your romantic commitments. Having a well-functioning marriage or dating relationship will do wonders for your mental health, regardless of what else is going in your professional life.

And speaking of romantic relationships, I hope this goes without saying, but it is an unambiguously bad idea to have a romantic relationship, either a casual hook-up or a serious love affair, with a faculty member in your department while you are in graduate school. Many universities have codes of conduct that regulate and frequently prohibit this kind of behavior. And while it is true that there have been successful long-term relationships between faculty and graduate students, it is also an empirical reality that for every successful relationship, there are 10 (I made that number up, but suffice it to say, many more) relationships that end badly, and it is always the case that it is the student who loses out in terms of her graduate school experience, scholarly reputation, and professional prospects.

If you find yourself stuck in this kind of dilemma, or some other kind, or perhaps find yourself depressed, unmotivated, anxious, or otherwise just not 100 percent, there are resources at the university that you can use. Although students are sometimes embarrassed or ashamed to seek the help of student counseling services, if you knew how many of your peers actually go to student counseling, you would not be embarrassed in the least. (My guess is that, at any given time, that number would include more than half the students in your program.) Seeing a counselor can be particularly helpful if you are concerned that the people around you may not always have your best interests at heart, or may respond badly if you tell them what you're really thinking. The most productive way to view your counselor is as an impartial friend to whom you can honestly disclose your thoughts and who may have helpful suggestions, but with the added benefit that there is no possibility of their blabbing what you tell them to other students, the faculty, or your family.

If seeing a counselor is still a bit too out there for you, see if there is a work-related discussion group you might join. Student services often set up dissertation writing groups in which students regularly meet to work on their dissertations and to talk about the writing process. Meeting with other students in different programs who are in the same boat can be helpful since you can commiserate and talk to sympathetic people. But be careful—some of these groups can turn into weekly group whines where nothing gets accomplished and people end up feeling worse than when they came in. Stay away from negative, disgruntled people. This is probably a good rule of thumb in general. You may not have much choice in having to do your dissertation, but you do have a choice in the kind of people with whom you surround yourself. A good litmus test is, if a person makes you feel worse—less sure of yourself, more worried, more depressed, more angry—stay away from that person.

In addition to having good personal relationships, the happiest people in grad school are those who are able to keep perspective about themselves and about school. A big mistake that many students make is to believe that if they don't do as well in grad school as they had hoped, they will be a Big Fat Failure in life.

Understand that you are more than your status as a graduate student. And you are certainly more than your status as an economist. Many students who enter graduate school in economics have only ever been students and have only ever done economics, so they cannot conceive of themselves doing something else or being happy doing something else. And when they find they are no longer the top dog in economics, they think their one chance for happiness and life satisfaction is over.

Phooey. Being a Ph.D. economist is a job, not a life calling. Yes, there are many good things about it, but you as a person are not defined by it. Your value and worth as a person have nothing to do with being an economist or where you are in the academic pecking order. You are much more important than that. And you have choices. You are still young, you are smart, you have lots of skills. Maybe this econ thing will work out, maybe it won't. Remind yourself that, regardless of what happens, you are a pretty cool person who will have a meaningful and happy life.

Should I Stay or Should I Go?

It is unusual for a student to go through grad school without at least a second of a doubt about whether this is the right thing for him to do. And there are many now-successful Ph.D. economists who had such doubts when they were in your position.

But how do you know whether your doubts are just run-of-the-mill insecurities or real red flags? It's entirely possible that *this particular graduate program* may not be right for you *at this particular moment* in your life. It doesn't mean that the program won't be right for you later on. Or that you might not be happier in another Ph.D. economics program. Many, many students, especially those who went straight from college to grad school, leave their program and later choose to return to the same or a different program, renewed and refreshed and doing well.

You may also be reassured—although admissions and program directors may be less reassured—to know that, for the latest cohort for which we have information, 28 percent of economics students had dropped out by the end of their second year (Stock, Siegfried, and Finegan 2011). That's right: just under a third of students who entered doctoral economics programs had dropped out within two years. To round out this picture, we also know from a separate earlier study that the ten-year completion rate, in other words the proportion of students who complete their Ph.D. within ten years, is around 52 percent (Council of Graduate Schools 2007). Since very few students finish after ten years, we can interpret this to mean that only slightly more than half of students who enter Ph.D. economics programs actually leave with a Ph.D. degree.

Why the high attrition rate and poor completion rate? We don't really know, but some conjectured reasons are: lack of mentorship, failure of the department to resolve conflicts between faculty and students, and unrealistic expectations on the part of students— although I hope this book will go some way toward alleviating this last problem.

Departments surely have some responsibility for helping their students successfully complete their programs. But it may also be that once you're in graduate school, you have more information about academic economics and what it takes to be an economist. And it is reasonable —and to be expected—that some students will question whether this is the right path for them at this point in their lives. So you are far from alone if you have these kinds of doubts.

With all the pressures of graduate work that can get you down, what you may need right now is a break. Not just any break, but a productive break where you can perhaps try some other possibilities and take a fresh look at where you are.

There are a number of ways to do this without dropping out altogether. First, you can take the summer to do something besides staying on campus. Be an intern at a bank, a think tank, or a start-up. Or do something completely different from economics (if you choose this route and are worried about what the faculty might think, then for gosh sakes, don't tell them). Find out what it's like to not be in school.

If you think you would like to stay in academia but perhaps move into a different program like public policy or law school, sit in on those classes to see what they are like. This way, you will be more informed and you will be in a better position if you do choose to go in that direction.

Another possibility is to visit another university. Many universities have exchange programs that allow their students to visit other schools. Visiting another department is incredibly informative in terms of figuring out whether the issues you have are with economics in general or with your program in particular. And the new university will have academic resources that your university may not have. Take advantage of the courses offered, within economics and outside economics. Talk to faculty and students (but don't trash talk your department) to get a different perspective.

Still another possibility is to request a leave of absence. This may be your only option if you are going to try something completely different. Two cautionary points regarding this route. First, in requesting your leave, it is probably not a good idea to mention that you are not sure about economics and would like to work in postmodern performance art for a while. Just put it down to family reasons. Don't say you're depressed or need a break. Unfortunately, there are reputational consequences to admitting emotional vulnerability, even among the most enlightened program directors (remember, these people are not your parents or your therapist). Just say that you have to help out with family matters but that you are planning to come back as soon as these issues get sorted out. Second, before taking a leave, make sure you have a plan for what you are going to do. Have the job or internship in hand. You want to have a productive leave, where you get the additional information that you need to decide whether to stay in the program or seek your fortune elsewhere.

A last possibility is to just gut things out with the hope of doing something different after you graduate. Some students, especially those who have passed their exams and have meandered through third year without a topic, choose this option. To be sure, there are many good job opportunities for Ph.D. economists outside of academia. If working as this kind of economist interests you, then the psychic, financial, and opportunity costs of spending the next three years of your life coughing up a good-enough dissertation may well be worth the benefits. Indeed, you may enjoy these graduate years of freedom and view getting a Ph.D. as a consumption good.

But don't stay in and finish the program simply because you've made it thus far, especially if you are interested in a career—for example, being an entrepreneur—that doesn't require a Ph.D. To me, this seems like a lot of work, effort, and grief to go through to end up doing something that did not require a dissertation; the principle of sunk cost would seem to apply here. Plus, remember that *having* a Ph.D. can lock you into certain kinds of jobs and out of other jobs; even if you are a zillion times smarter and more analytically adroit than the non-Ph.D. job candidates, some employers will be reluctant to hire a Ph.D. graduate for jobs that typically go to M.B.A.s. Thus, Ph.D. jobs frequently pay far less than jobs not requiring a Ph.D. If you would like to be an economic consultant or work at a tech desk in an investment firm, great. But if your professional goals can be met without a Ph.D., get out as soon as you can, so you can start investing in your new life.

One last note. By getting to where you are now, you have shown that you have the brains and technical skills to do well in many different professions. Many times, students undervalue who they are and what skills they have because they have always been in environments where the professors know so much and the students are left to feel that they know so little. Out in the real world, you will find that the skills you have are scarce and highly valued, and you can find jobs that will pay you very very well for what you know. Do a bit of research to find out what it is you would like to do and who would be willing to pay you to do it. For ideas on how to go about this process, see Basalla and Debelius 2007.

Finally, even if you have decided to leave and do something completely different forever and ever, don't burn any bridges. You may feel angry or resentful at the program for mistreating you, and you may want to tell people off, for their good and for the improvement of the program. Don't. Leave graciously. The past is the past, and you have a new life to lead.

References

Basalla, Susan, and Maggie Debelius. 2007. *"So What Are You Going to Do with That?": Finding Careers Outside Academia.* Chicago: University of Chicago Press.

Council of Graduate Schools. 2007. *Ph.D. Completion and Attrition: Analysis of Baseline Program Data from the Ph.D. Completion Project.* Washington, D.C.: Council of Graduate Schools.

Stock, Wendy A., John J. Siegfried, and T. Aldrich Finegan. 2011. "Completion Rates and Time-to-Degree in Economics Ph.D. Programs." *American Economic Association Papers and Proceedings* 101: 176–187.

Further Reading

Stock, Wendy A., T. Aldrich Finegan, and John J. Siegfried. 2006. "Attrition in Economics Ph.D. Programs." *American Economic Association Papers and Proceedings* 96: 458–465.

Stock, Wendy A., T. Aldrich Finegan, and John J. Siegfried. 2009. "Completing an Economics Ph.D. in Five Years." *American Economic Association Papers and Proceedings* 99: 624–629.

Stock, Wendy A., and John J. Siegfried. 2006. "Time-to-Degree for the Economics Ph.D. Class of 2001–2002." *American Economic Association Papers and Proceedings* 96: 467–474.

Chapter 7

Thrown In with the Sharks: Women and International Students

It is an empirical statement, not a political statement, to say that the majority of faculty and students in economics departments at U.S. universities are American males. This simple fact has implications for students who are not in this category. At the very least, you may feel self-conscious about the fact that you are non-male or non-American in a sea of American maleness. At worst, you may be forced to deal with repugnant behavior stemming from retrograde attitudes and beliefs or from the social clumsiness of the demographic majority. In other words, if you are female or a student from overseas, you will face not only the intellectual, social, and psychological challenges that I've highlighted in the previous chapters, but some additional hurdles as well. This is not to say that American males don't face their own set of problems, and we can certainly shed (a few) tears for them. This chapter, however, is about those who are not in the disciplinary demographic majority, and acknowledges that some of the advice given in this book thus far should be adapted or supplemented to suit their particular cases.

Although the concerns of women and international students are combined in this chapter, these two populations do not face exactly the same issues. There are of course similarities—for example, having to face discriminatory behavior—but in an effort not to muddy things up or overgeneralize to the point of being unhelpful, I address the concerns of these two distinct student populations in separate sections.

Women

Although more women are entering the economics profession, the preponderance of faculty and students is still male. Moreover, within economics, women disproportionately cluster in certain subfields such as labor and development, and are relatively sparse in, say, monetary policy or financial economics. To the extent that you are aware of feeling different or believe that you are treated differently because of your gender, this experience will be more acute in subfields with fewer women. It also would not be a stretch to say, although some may disagree, that on average you can observe more aggressive, boorish, and on occasion sexist behavior in those subfields where there are more men.

In giving advice, there are two ways to think about the problems faced by female students in male-dominated fields like economics. One is to consider the behaviors that will lead to an optimal outcome for the individual female student, and the other is to consider the behaviors that will lead to an optimal outcome for the system as a whole. I take the first approach—focusing on the individual—primarily because it is the job of this book to get you, the individual student, to successfully complete the Ph.D. program. While I would also like to make the world a less unfair and less discriminatory place, that is not this book's primary objective, and I will concede that what might be optimal for the individual may not lead the system to a better equilibrium in which all would benefit. This individualistic approach is driven primarily by the sad but very real fact that you, as a student, are not exactly in a position of power in graduate school or in the profession; you are dependent on the goodwill of the faculty and on the department's purse strings. You can of course try to shake things up, but there may be a professional price to pay even if you are able to enact some changes, and only you can do the cost-benefit calculation to see whether this price is worth it.

The most immediate problem you may encounter upon entering graduate school is prejudice and discrimination from your peers—mostly from males but on occasion from other females. Many male economics students have some version of a narcissistic personality disorder wherein they think that most other students are dumber than they are. Bear in mind that they also think most other male students are dumber than they are, but you may experience their contempt as sexism since it is often directed specifically at female students, who they believe have an easier time through the admissions process. Some male students have particular difficulty with attractive females, believing that it is physically impossible to be smart and pretty at the same time, and that surely these women have used (and will use) their feminine wiles to get ahead. It is also not uncommon to see this attitude among your female classmates. In addition, you may find these discriminatory beliefs reflected in the behaviors of your male professors, although rather than feeling resentful of your perceived privileges (which you supposedly have because you are female), the faculty may be more inclined to behave in a condescending way.

This is a long way of saying that, at some point in your graduate life, you may have to deal with people who think you have gotten to where you are, not by brains or competence or hard work, but by some assumed privileges associated with being female. Perhaps they assume that you are a beneficiary of affirmative action policies or that your feminine charms have hoodwinked legions of male reference letter writers. People may ignore you, interrupt you, dismiss your research, and engage in all manner of rude behavior. The point is, these prior beliefs about you as an individual, based on your membership in the female gender, are dismissive of your ability and achievement.

Is there anything that can be done to combat this irrational prejudice or (at best) statistical discrimination? There is a large scholarly literature in economics and sociology on gender discrimination, and others are far more qualified than I to advise you on the best course of action to change the system. I am only here to advise you on how to get through the graduate program successfully despite this un-pleasantness. To this end, I have four different pieces of advice. The first three involve (slowly) changing people's prior beliefs; the last involves making the most of a constrained situation.

1. *Be really, really good.* There is no substitute for being a really good economist. Of course, this advice applies equally to male and female graduate students, but it is particularly helpful for female students. If you are good technically, if you are creative with your research ideas, if you are an independent thinker, if you are able to marshal your efforts into a coherent, publishable paper—no one can argue with that, no matter which set of reproductive organs you have. Unfortunately, it may be the case that you have to be *better* than a man to get to the same place, and no, this isn't fair. But stay focused on your endgame, which is to be a first-rate economist.

2. *Speak up.* One error that female graduate students often make is to blend into the background and wait to be noticed. They think that if they do all the right things (and even if they follow my first commandment of being really, really good), then they will be noticed and anointed. This may or may not happen. But one way to ensure that you are noticed for your brains is to engage with others and speak up. Ask questions, clarify confusing claims, contribute to the intellectual conversation instead of just smiling and nodding politely.

3. *Do not play the gender card.* I'm sure we all know of female students who bat their eyes at brainy young men and feign interest in them so that they can get help on their problem sets or get attention for reasons other than their economic competence. This is exactly the kind of behavior that reinforces the discrimination and stereotyping that professional women fight so hard against. Unfortunately, you can't play it both ways. These men are your professional colleagues, not simply means to satisfy your ego needs for affirmation of your physical attractiveness. Act like a professional. A

good rule of thumb is to treat everyone as if he were your (younger) brother.

4. *Don't throw your pearls before swine.* By this I mean, there will be some people whom you just can't please. There will be some dinosaurs, both among the faculty and among the male students, who prefer to view women in an archaic light. Don't bother trying to win them over. Of course, be as good as you can be and don't be intimidated by them, but don't waste your time getting frustrated at yourself because you can't convince them to see you with clarity. There are plenty of enlightened faculty out there—both male and female— who would be happy to advise a smart, ambitious, female graduate student.

Sexual Harassment

Although the targets of sexual harassment can be male or female, gay or straight, the primary targets in a predominantly heterosexual male environment like an economics department tend to be younger female graduate students. It goes without saying but I'll say it anyway: unwanted sexual attention is *verboten*. Under no circumstances is it appropriate for a faculty member to make unwanted sexual advances toward a graduate student or to impose any sexual conditions on a student's course grade or on any other part of her academic evaluation. The tricky part, of course, is to make clear to the faculty member that his advances are indeed unwanted so that he stops harassing you, but to avoid embarrassing him, so that he doesn't professionally punish you. You may find him deeply repulsive or just generally creepy, but you can't really come out and say so.

The best approach is to be polite but direct, and to respond in a way that is commensurate with the offense. If he simply starts saying inappropriate or highly personal things (e.g., his wife doesn't understand him, his marriage is in trouble), nod politely if sympathetically but don't otherwise respond. Don't engage or ask for elaboration. It's best that you appear nonplussed by his overtures but at the same time not encourage him to pursue the conversation he wishes to have. He may be testing the waters and your receptiveness with over-disclosure, and if there is an awkward silence and perhaps a furrowing of your brow, he will get the hint. You may have to use this awkward silence approach a couple of times if he is the persistent type.

One danger with crossing a faculty member who engages in harassment is that he can become enraged at your rejection, no matter how politely your refusal is expressed. Although you cannot with 100 percent certainty prevent retaliation, you can try to diminish this possibility by remaining friendly and polite when you see him; don't give him any hope that you'll give in, of course, but don't ignore him completely as that will enrage him further.

Some people may disagree with this advice. Perhaps it encourages women to be too polite or docile, and it lets the harasser off the hook. If you disagree with this advice, I would welcome your alternative suggestions (see Chapter 9 for contact information). The strategies should not have negative consequences for the student. Actual past cases would be most helpful.

Regardless of how the harassment goes down, you should *immediately* report any such incident, ideally to an officer at your university designated to deal with sexual harassment. Even if you eventually choose not to file a formal complaint, it is crucial that there is documentation of these incidents so that if the offender retaliates against you, you will have some way of defending yourself. And it probably helps (although not always in a legal sense) to tell a few trusted friends at the time of the incident.

You can bet that a faculty member who is willing to hit on you in this way and abuse his power is not doing this for the first time. These faculty members have reputations, and longtime administrative assistants and female faculty will be most knowledgeable about this kind of thing. You may find it helpful to seek affirmation or advice from them should you find yourself to be the target of harassment, but it can be difficult to identify which people you can trust to respond sensitively. If you confide in the "wrong" person, you may get blamed for having been the victim, or word could spread in a way that is difficult for you to control. While you might think that it would be a good thing to get the word out about the faculty member's boorish behavior, it may well exacerbate the situation if the faculty member feels threatened enough to punish you for embarrassing him.

Social Support

Some women find it helpful to talk to other women about the gender issues they face in academia, and almost all universities have student support groups for these kinds of concerns. I have found, however, that in economics departments, there are relatively few such institutionalized settings for social support on gender issues, as compared to, say, in sociology or psychology departments or in the humanities or even the natural sciences.

Indeed, many female economics faculty would deny that they have ever felt discriminated against because of their gender, and some—especially the more senior female faculty who have achieved tenure—discount gender issues as a concern in the profession. Researchers (mostly women) who study gender-related issues, such as economics of the family or gender discrimination, are considered to be too narrowly specialized or too ideological or emotional. And there may be a perception that students who complain about how women are treated in economics or in the economics program are whiners or troublemakers. In short, there seems to be greater hostility or at best indifference to the problems that women in particular face in the economics profession, perhaps because economic theory finds it very difficult to explain continued discrimination against any group if it entails a productivity cost.

I mention these attitudes to raise your awareness of the difficulty you may have in finding social support, even among women, for the gender-related issues that you may encounter. Some female faculty may be excellent mentors to women, but you should not assume that simply because a professor is female she will be sympathetic to your concerns. In fact, some male professors may make better mentors—not because they themselves face these issues, but because they are more reflective about the social and professional environment of the field.

If you find you would like to talk about gender-related concerns, your best first step may be to find sympathetic female graduate students. These students, especially those in cohorts ahead of you, will then be able to identify sympathetic faculty. Obviously, researchers who work on topics related to gender discrimination are also good candidates for discussing gender issues. You may have to go outside your department or even your university to find the social and professional support you need; the American Economic Association's Committee on the Status of Women in the Economics Profession can help you identify economists who are engaged with gender issues in the discipline.

In summary, as a woman you may face additional hurdles that can impede your progress in your economics graduate program. In some ways, fair or not, you need to be more careful about your professional and social behavior. But there is support at your university and in the profession for the concerns of women economists, and I would urge that you seek out the people and organizations who can provide that support.

International Students

Going through a graduate program in economics can be difficult, but I won't lie—going through a graduate program in economics as an international student can be *very* difficult. Let me recount the additional ways in which your life can be that much more arduous.

- If you are not a native English-speaker, you will spend much of your first year bewildered and frustrated by things said or done around you that you do not fully comprehend.
- Your peers, teachers, and students (not to mention the service people and others with whom you have to interact on a daily basis) may have difficulty understanding you. You may not be

able to fully express what you are thinking and may be repeatedly misunderstood. When people don't understand you they may ask you to repeat things, or worse, ignore you.

- You may not be clear on what is expected (and not expected) of you as a student, or what is reasonable to expect from a faculty member, because of cultural differences between the United States and your home country.
- You may be discriminated against or mocked or treated poorly because of your cultural and ethnic difference. You may be exploited or taken advantage of by others because of both your relative inexperience in the U.S. academic environment and your reluctance to complain.
- If you work as a TA, your students may have difficulty understanding you. You may also be less effective as a teacher than you want to be because of different expectations regarding the student-teaching assistant relationship. Students may complain about you to the faculty.
- Without family or friends nearby, you may feel socially isolated in this new environment, and have difficulty making friends or finding people with whom you have much in common. You may feel you have no one to talk to or confide in.
- If your spouse and children accompany you to the United States, you may have to support them on your limited student stipend. This financial hardship may generate additional stress in your life and strain your relationship with your spouse.

On the plus side, however, the one thing you can almost always be sure of is that you are probably technically better prepared than most American students in the program. There are two reasons for this, as I mentioned in Chapter 3. One is that undergraduate programs overseas are generally more focused and more technically advanced than U.S. undergraduate economics programs. The undergraduate coursework in overseas programs is concentrated on economics, while American undergraduate programs include courses in many other areas, so American students have less exposure to economics as a whole, and less exposure to the kind of economics that will be done in graduate school. A second reason is that international students are probably held to a higher standard for admission than American students. Overseas programs and faculty letter writers are not often personally known to those reviewing graduate school applications, so international students are considered more of a risk. One way to deal with this additional risk is to admit only students who are superstars in their home country, or who are recommended by overseas faculty with international reputations. For these reasons, you as an international student will be far more prepared for graduate coursework than many of your American classmates.

An additional cause for optimism is that, despite all the difficulties that I have outlined, many international students have come before you and have done well. At a minimum, they have brought back with them a first-rate graduate education and a solid degree that opens professional doors. Many have not only survived but have thrived, as evidenced by the sizable number of international faculty in U.S. economics departments today. The payoff is well worth it.

Having said that, there is no need to go through more trouble and pain than you absolutely have to. If you are prepared for what lies ahead, you can take action to minimize the difficulties that you will encounter.

Language Difficulties

If you are not a native speaker of English, your first months in the United States will be stressful. Your brain will be on overload as you adapt to thinking and speaking in a different language, not to mention trying to cope with graduate work. It is natural to be fearful of making mistakes and to avoid speaking in English and looking foolish, but it is crucial that you become comfortable in English, in order to move ahead in graduate school and also subsequently in your career, since most of academic economics is conducted in English. Get as much practice speaking in English as possible; although you may be fearful of making mistakes, the courage and investment up-front will have immense payoffs. Take advantage of conversational English courses and practice groups offered at your university. In addition to their educational value, these are also a good way to meet other students who are facing the same linguistic and academic stresses as you.

Practice in speaking English helps you expand your vocabulary, understand more of what is being said, and think more quickly in the foreign language, but an underappreciated aspect of speaking a second language involves making yourself clearly understood in tone (i.e., whether you are happy, angry, or bored) and not just content. If the speech sounds, stress patterns (i.e., which syllables are emphasized), and intonation (i.e., which syllables have high or low pitch) of your native language are very different from that of American English, there are more possibilities for you and your intentions to be misinterpreted. In my experience, a person's speech stress patterns and intonation are disproportionately a cause of communication failure, rather than using the wrong word or making grammatical mistakes. People can accommodate errors in word selection when conversing with a non-native speaker, but misinterpretations caused by errors in syllable stresses and intonation are difficult to identify and overcome. For example, frequent syllable stresses may be a standard feature of the speaker's native language, but are interpreted as hostility or anger in English spoken language. I would recommend that students who are not native speakers of English, in addition to pursuing opportunities to practice conversational English, also take an accent reduction class. There are subtle aspects of meaning that are expressed through English syllable stresses and intonation, and being aware of these and in control of them is an important but often neglected part of speaking English as a second language.

Teaching Difficulties

A common complaint in economics departments is that the teaching assistants (also sometimes the faculty) don't speak English. There are usually two meanings to this. One is that they "speak" mostly using math. This issue is pervasive throughout the discipline and

I don't have much to say about this. The second meaning, which is the meaning most relevant to this chapter, is that students have difficulty understanding their non-native-English-speaking instructors. I hope that the previous section on language difficulties addresses some of this. Here, I elaborate on additional strategies.

If you know that people have difficulty understanding your accent—and even if people do not have difficulty understanding you—it helps to start your class by acknowledging to students that sometimes they may not understand everything you say, because of language differences or, say, because you speak quickly or go through the material rapidly. You need not express the issue as a deficiency on your part (which some graduate students are averse to doing, especially if they are concerned about conveying sufficient authority). Simply state as an empirical fact the possibility that students may not understand you, and let them know that they can ask you to repeat things or ask questions if that happens. This way, students—even if they do have difficulty understanding you—will be less inclined to be hostile toward you, and will perceive you as being sensitive to their needs and concerns. This, in turn, will prevent student complaints about you to the department.

Another common complaint about TAs from overseas is that they are not very helpful. There is an expectation among some American undergraduates that instructors are supposed to tell them exactly how to solve a problem or answer a homework question. You may come from a teaching tradition where you had to figure out your own solutions (and in fact this is how you got to where you are as a graduate student). You may even feel that giving students answers is not your job; your primary task is to lecture on relevant topics and grade student assignments, not to solve the problems for students that they need to solve for themselves. Be aware that this difference in expectations can be a source of tension between you and your students. The best suggestion I have for this problem is to seek guidance from the faculty member who is responsible for the course. Faculty differ in how much assistance they expect you to give students. If the faculty instructor is fine with your showing students step-by-step how to do something, then go ahead and do this, even if it feels uncomfortable to you. If, on the other hand, he has views similar to yours in terms of letting students work on their own, then be clear to the students that you will not be giving them answers because the faculty member teaching the course does not want you to do so. This way, if students have complaints about not being given answers, they need to address the issue with the primary faculty member.

You may notice that students eat in class, come and go whenever they like, sleep at their desks, surf on their laptops, text on their phones, and in general do all manner of rude things during class. This behavior may come as a shock to you if you come from a system where teachers are treated with respect and deference. In the United States, it would be a huge mistake to assume that you automatically get respect simply because you are the instructor; for better or worse, a more egalitarian relationship between students and instructors is something that you should get used to. As an instructor, you can of course impose rules such as no laptops or phone use during class, and can expect students to be quiet (even if not attentive) while you're lecturing, but expect little more than formal adherence to your rules.

Student-Faculty Relationships

Just as the relationship between your students and you is more casual than in your home country, the relationship between you and the faculty in your department will be more informal as well. Many American professors, especially the younger ones, are uncomfortable with being called "Professor" and prefer being addressed by their first names—although it's always prudent to ask faculty first how they would like to be addressed. There is much more of a friendly relationship between faculty and students, as opposed to one characterized by deference to authority, although you should bear in mind that faculty do wield quite a bit of authority (e.g., dissertation decisions, reference letter writing) so it is best to act professionally around them.

If there are faculty in the department from your home country, you should make an effort to meet them and get to know them, even if they are working in a completely different field. Although obviously simply being from the same country or speaking the same language does not mean that you will find them congenial or interesting, it never hurts to establish some kind of relationship with these faculty; you already have something in common and these faculty can be a resource for determining whether any issues you are encountering are simply cultural differences, or are a sign of a greater problem.

Social Support

Graduate school can be difficult, and it is important to have friends or some kind of social support system to make the rough periods more bearable. Study groups are often formed with those who share a nationality or who speak the same language. While there are costs and benefits to these kinds of study groups intellectually and professionally, people find them helpful socially because the cultural similarity means there is one less stress to worry about. Even if you find your fellow students from your home country odd or not at all compatible, it is still helpful to maintain some ties with them, if only to have some connection with the familiar as you navigate your new environment.

If there are no others in your department from your home country, talk to your university's international programs office, which can be helpful in identifying other students from your country of origin or informing you about student organizations that might be of interest. These offices also often organize international student social activities, and you may find that talking to international students, regardless of their home country, can be useful in helping you adjust to the United States.

Finally, you may consider going to your university counseling center if you need to confide in someone about problems, both personal and professional, that you are facing. Although in many countries there is a stigma associated with seeing a counselor or a therapist, paying a visit to a school psychologist is fairly common (and considered healthy) in the United States, and many graduate students take advantage of these services in the course of their program.

The Job Market

Although international students have a relative advantage in the coursework stage of the program, they are often at a relative disadvantage on the job market. There are several reasons for this. First, there is a great deal of stereotyping and statistical discrimination that happens during the first stage of the recruitment process. At this stage, review committees assess the candidates on paper (i.e., through their vita, job market paper, and letters of recommendation), and make quick decisions based on perhaps superficial characteristics. If you have a name that reflects that you are from a region whose students have traditionally had difficulty being understood in English, then regardless of your own language ability, prospective employers will (unfairly) assume language complications. Letters of recommendation from advisors confirming your language ability can be important in alleviating this concern, but the first-stage assessments are done so quickly that this piece of information may be overlooked. Some students Anglicize their names or choose "American" names to put on their vitas to signal their facility with English language and culture, and this is not necessarily a bad idea.

Some students also come from countries that have a reputation for producing technically proficient but uncreative economists. Or from countries that have a known ideological bias. Or from countries which have some other reputation over which you have absolutely no control. Statistical discrimination will be a problem for you, and your letters of reference will be an important way for recruiters to adjust their beliefs about you as a candidate. But again, the first cut for interviews happens very quickly, so some important information conveyed in these letters may be missed.

Also, since you are not an American citizen, U.S. employers know that they have to go through additional paperwork to justify your employment. For this reason, many employers, especially those who are not used to hiring non-U.S. citizens, will be more reluctant to give you an interview. You may have a somewhat better chance with American employers that have international offices, or that work on topics that have an international focus, and can benefit from your background and language skills.

The end result for international students, nevertheless, is that your job market paper and letters of reference (and your graduate program) will have to be that much better for you to secure an interview with a U.S. employer. For academic jobs in particular, international students need to be relative superstars in their programs to get a U.S. placement.

While it is fine to have high aspirations, it is also sensible to have some kind of insurance policy so that you don't leave the job market empty-handed. You will likely have the best chance of getting a job in your home country, and as a job candidate from an American program, you will be in a good position to land quite a good job. So apply also to a reasonable range of jobs in your home country in case your applications in the United States do not work out.

Since you will be in the United States when you are applying for jobs, there are things you can do to increase your chance of securing a job offer in your own country. First, talk to faculty in your department who are from your country. They will have the best insider knowledge of the job market, people, and employers, and will be a good source for advice. Second, talk to faculty in your subfield at other American universities who are from your home country. It is best to develop these relationships one or two years before you go on the market; presumably you will have been talking to researchers in your field about your dissertation and will already have developed these ties. In general, it's not as helpful to contact researchers outside your university just as you enter the market if you have never met or talked to them before (the only exception is if one of your advisors puts you in touch with someone she knows). In addition, you will want to develop relationships with faculty in your home country who work in your subfield. Your undergraduate or master's degree advisors, who are probably the faculty who wrote your letters of reference, may also be able to help you at this stage.

Finally, presumably there are central sites for economics job candidates in your home country. Each country's economic association will obviously differ in how they handle this, so this is something you will have to research on your own.

I realize that there is a great deal of heterogeneity in international students' experiences of graduate school, depending on the competitiveness of their department, whether they did their undergraduate studies in the United States, and so on. I would welcome comments and suggestions from international students based on their own experiences (see Chapter 9 for contact information).

The main lesson from this chapter is that, yes, as an international student you have more challenges as you go through your graduate program and as you navigate the job market. That said, if you persevere and try to learn as much as you can—intellectually, culturally, linguistically, professionally—you will be in a very good position when you graduate and in the years to come.

Further Reading

Aslanbeigui, Nahid, and Veronica Montecinos. 1998. "Foreign Students in U.S. Doctoral Programs." *Journal of Economic Perspectives* 12: 171–182.

Chapter 8

Getting a Job: Taking Your Show on the Road

While the first year may be the worst year of grad school, the last year may well be its most stressful. Now that you've got the hang of this grad school thing, you are now being asked, with very little guidance, to find yourself a job. After spending an inordinate amount of time working on your job market paper and submitting it to what seems like ten thousand places, you will spend an inordinate amount sitting around waiting for things to happen and people to call you. If all goes well, people will judge you and talk about you behind your back and eventually make you a job offer. All this waiting and judging and uncertainty can wreak havoc on even the most stable personalities.

Although Ph.D. job markets are always a bit dicey, be reassured that we are in a discipline where the market mostly clears: almost everyone gets a job. You may not always get your first-choice job (welcome to the real world), and you may not get to live in your ideal location, but you will more than likely be employed.

A useful way to view the job market is that it is both a coming-out party (in the debutante sense) and a beauty pageant. It is a coming-out party in the sense that you are being formally introduced to the profession. There are certain expectations for your behavior and rituals you must perform, and this is the way for the profession to get to know you. In addition, the job market is like a beauty pageant in the sense that people will be looking you over and evaluating you on the basis of what they perceive to be desirable features. As with many beauty pageants, some very attractive candidates do less well than expected, and some candidates who don't appear to be that much better than the others do extraordinarily well.

These analogies suggest that you should prepare for the job market seriously but that you should not take the outcome too seriously. You should write the best job market paper that you possibly can and do your best to prepare for your job talk and interviews because you are showing yourself off to the profession. At the same time, because the market can be quirky and hard to predict, your job market outcome should not be viewed as an official verdict on your value or potential as an economist.

When to Go on the Job Market

Most students go on the market during the fall of their fifth or sixth year. I would suggest going earlier rather than later. Students *always* feel unprepared and are often tempted to wait an additional year so they can feel really ready. Some advisors may even encourage students to defer, but bear in mind that advisors get the benefit of your doing well on the market (with a better paper if you defer) but don't pay the cost of your deferring (forgone income and getting on with your life) so their incentives are very different from yours. Of course, if your advisor feels strongly that you are not ready, you should do what she says since she may write a less enthusiastic letter than she otherwise might have.

If you have more of a laissez-faire advisor who lets you choose your own timing, you should go on the market when you have a paper that is publishable. That is to say, you have your main result and have done most of the ancillary work to support that main result (you will never have done *all* of the supplemental work because someone will always think of something else you can do). The only good reasons to defer are if you have a project but no results (i.e., you have no paper), or if you will absolutely have a blockbuster paper (and not just the hope of a blockbuster paper) if you wait one more year. You will learn much more in your first couple of years as an independent researcher than in the equivalent amount of time in an extended grad school experience, so it's always better to get a real job sooner rather than later.

Your paper should be in a prepared state by the end of the summer. Because the application process is time-consuming, it will be extremely stressful for you to be making major revisions to your paper while you are writing cover letters and research statements and submitting applications. Of course, you can do additional work on the project (ancillary analyses, robustness checks), but these analyses are for your own information. You can mention this supplementary work in job market talks or in casual discussion, but there is no need to keep revising the job market paper. You can incorporate the additions into a new version of your paper later on, after your job search is over. For your own sanity, unless you find a terrible and obvious error that overturns all your results, set a date for yourself at the end of the summer when you will stop working on your paper.

Another option that is becoming more popular is to graduate "early" (in your fifth or even your fourth year) and instead of going on the market in the fall of your last Ph.D. year, apply for postdoctoral fellowships. A staple in the natural sciences, postdocs have become much more popular in the social sciences in recent years. These are short-term positions that provide one or two years of time after your Ph.D. to do research. But be careful, not all postdocs are alike. Many of the most desirable and most competitive postdocs, such as the Harvard Society of Fellows, the Robert Wood Johnson Health Policy Scholars program, and the Stanford Institute for Economic and Policy Research fellowship, give you the freedom to pursue your own research. Other postdoc fellowships, however, require you to spend some time working on a specific project, using a specific data set, working for a particular professor, or teaching. Postdocs that are constrained in this way are not ideal because you will have little time to work on your own research. And with the exception of the top fellowships, postdocs do not pay particularly well. On the other hand, postdocs give you the opportunity to spend time at a different institution and develop your professional connections. They are a particularly good option if you plan to specialize in experimental economics or in the kinds of "big data" empirical studies discussed in Chapter 5. In these cases, you can make very good use of the postdoc time working on a specific dataset or set of experiments or apprenticing with a different professor. Because the training and the projects in these areas of economics have longer time frames, postdocs are a natural way for you to develop the additional technical skills required to work in these specialized areas.

More generally—even if you are not an experimentalist or a "big data" person—if you are able to secure a good postdoc with protected research time, you will be able to develop a stronger publishing record and may benefit in terms of a better placement because of this. For this reason, more students in top- and mid-ranked departments are now choosing to defer going on the market until after they have completed a postdoc.

The Mechanics of the Job Market Process

So what actually happens in this thing called the economics job market? Here is a quick overview. Beginning in August, departments start placing ads for assistant professor positions (and lecturer and visiting positions) in a monthly publication produced by the American Economic Association (AEA) called Job Openings for Economists (JOE). Consulting firms, research and policy organizations, government agencies, and any other place that hires Ph.D. economists will also advertise their positions there. Most openings are listed in the September and October issues of JOE.

These ads will ask that you send your curriculum vitae and your job market paper and have three letters of reference sent under separate cover. Even if employers do not request it, is also good form to send them a brief (one-page) cover letter describing yourself, your job market paper, and your research interests. By the way, when I say that you will be asked to send documents, that can mean one of three things. You may be asked to upload the documents at an application website designated by the employer for the position (often a standard application website used by their university). Or you may be asked to upload the documents at a website called econjobmarket.org. At this website, which is a nonprofit organization run by academic economists, you only need to upload your vita and your job market paper once. You can then designate multiple departments that are to be sent your documents. Your professors can also upload your reference letters through this website. Or finally, old school-style, you may occasionally be asked to send a hard copy of the documents to a departmental address.

Most ads will indicate a deadline sometime in November. If the ad does not have a deadline listed or has a very late deadline, do not be fooled. Applications need to be reviewed in time for the AEA meetings in early January, so you should always try to get your application in by Thanksgiving.

Your department will typically hold a meeting or a series of meetings at the beginning of the fall term for students going on the market. At this meeting, they will introduce you to the placement director(s) and brief you on the mechanics of how your specific department handles the job market process (e.g., reference letters). You will also have an opportunity to ask any job market questions you may have.

In the middle of the fall, faculty hold a meeting in which they discuss all the candidates in the department who are on the market that year. Although departments vary in exactly how they do this, it is during this meeting that faculty rank the department's (top) candidates and discuss placements that are likely or possible based on the candidates' job market papers and research areas. At this meeting, your advisor will play an important role in describing you, your paper, and your research or teaching interests.

For better or worse, this super-secret meeting can determine the scope of your academic job opportunities for this season. In many departments, especially the top and upper-middle departments, initial interview decisions come through informal networks (i.e., faculty from your department gossiping about you to their friends in other departments), so the impression that faculty get about you from this meeting limits which departments will consider you, at least initially, a good prospect for them. More information may be revealed over time—who turns out to be oversold and undersold— but who gets on the AEA list of interviews obviously circumscribes who can potentially be invited out for a campus visit.

In departments where informal networks play less of a role (mostly lower-middle departments), the placement director is more important, but again she gets her information about students from this meeting as well. If a department is recruiting in a specific field, it asks the placement director for the names of candidates working in that field; the placement director then informs the querying department about candidates who are working in that field *and* who the department has decided will suit the rank of the recruiting department.

There are a few exceptions where you can have direct input. Liberal arts colleges might ask the placement director who among their candidates is particularly interested in and good at teaching undergraduates, or is looking for a more balanced teaching-research environment. Or consulting firms might ask the director who is interested in a private sector job. For this reason, you should make sure that your advisor and the placement director know if you have specific non-research professional preferences such as teaching or the private sector.

After all applications are submitted, search committees at the recruiting departments convene to decide on whom they would like to interview at the AEA annual meetings in early January. For every position they have open, departments typically interview ten to twenty candidates at the AEA meetings (more below). Based on these initial interviews, the departments usually issue flyout invitations to three or four candidates for each open position. Most flyouts are scheduled during January, February, and early March. Shortly thereafter, offers are made. Departments initially make an offer to their top choice among the flyout candidates; if that candidate declines their offer, they may issue another offer to a lower-ranked candidate, or may choose to not make additional offers and to wait until the next recruiting season.

How Many Applications

The typical candidate on the job market submits between 80 and 120 applications. For the average candidate, if he applies widely among different kinds and rankings of employers, this number of applications will likely result in ten to fifteen AEA interviews.

This means that, yes, 90 percent of applications ex post turn out to be a waste of time, postage, and clicking. We could save a lot of time and energy if each candidate applied to many fewer jobs. The problem is, it's difficult to know ex ante which of the applications will be a waste of time.

In an ideal world, to save you the effort of submitting pointless applications, you would have an honest conversation with your advisor about where she thinks you are likely to end up. Some advisors will be brutally honest and say, I'm not going to write you a letter for any department ranked above X. While this is helpful and certainly saves you time in focusing your applications, students tend to feel hurt and betrayed by such an attitude from an advisor. They think, does my advisor think I'm that bad? Or, my advisor doesn't have enough faith in me. Or, my advisor has just screwed up my chances of getting a good job and my life is ruined forever. Even if the advisor is very experienced and absolutely right about a student's likely placement, it is very difficult to have this conversation without hurting the student's feelings; no one wants to be the bad guy. Consequently many advisors tell their students to apply everywhere, and thus we have students applying willy-nilly to 150 places, some of which will not even read their applications.[1]

Nonetheless, there *is* a great deal of randomness in the job market process, which is a valid reason for many advisors to encourage their students to apply everywhere. Even the requested fields that are stated in the ads are sometimes misleading. These fields may often reflect wishful thinking rather than a real constraint. Without being in the departmental meetings yourself, it is very difficult to know exactly what a department wants. The department itself often does not know what it wants, and there may be different factions who want different things. Since you as a candidate are unlikely to know about these internal machinations, the job market application process really is a numbers game at least initially, and it is in your interest to apply widely.

Signaling and the Job Market Scramble

There have been two recent innovations in the economics job market that reflect attempts to reduce market inefficiencies. These innovations include a system in which candidates can send signals to indicate their interest to potential employers, and a late-season job marketplace aptly called the "scramble."

In the signaling system, candidates may choose to send, through JOE and the AEA, signals to up to two different employers in early December to indicate their particular interest in these employers. Because employers, in choosing candidates to interview, can make mistakes in identifying which applicants would be most interested in them (for example, believing that a candidate from a high-ranking university is unattainable), signals are a credible way for candidates to convey information about their interest.

There are several rules of thumb that have developed related to the effective use of signals as a way of securing interviews. In general, you send signals to departments that might not otherwise think you are a good fit, but for which you think you are a good fit (for personal reasons unobserved to them). This most frequently happens if the school does not normally recruit from, or has not hired from, your graduating department. Some lower-ranking schools may be inclined to believe that you are unattainable for them, and your sending a signal is a good way to indicate that you are genuinely interested (because of, say, spousal or family constraints, geographic preferences, or lifestyle reasons that are unobserved to them) instead of just using them as a safety school.

A second rule of thumb is that you should signal to liberal arts colleges if you are interested in teaching and research in a liberal arts environment but are graduating from a department that is not known for sending students to liberal arts colleges. Again, these colleges would tend to assume a low level of interest from you, and a signal would reflect some private information about your preferences. (It may however be more efficient to save your signals and have your letter writers indicate this in their letters to liberal arts colleges, but not all faculty can be bothered to send different letters to different institutions.)

Other rules of thumb include signaling to universities in less popular geographic regions, to nonacademic employers if you are graduating from a department that emphasizes academic placements, or to non-U.S. employers. Although these all seem like plausible uses of signals, their presumed effect on securing interviews has yet to be affirmed by the data, as reported by Coles et al. 2010.

The second innovation is the creation of the job market scramble, which begins in mid-March, after the main round of campus visits and hiring has taken place. Some departments find themselves with still open positions and many candidates find themselves without offers after this main round. This secondary market provides another opportunity for matches. Anecdotal evidence suggests that these positions tend to be short-term (i.e., visiting) positions or teaching-intensive positions at lower-ranked institutions. In any case, there are often far more job candidates than positions available, so if you do not have an offer by the start of the scramble, odds are that you are going to have to stay in graduate school for another year.

More details about signaling, the scramble, and other market design aspects of the economics job market may be found in the Coles et al. (2010) paper I mentioned above. I highly recommend that you read this paper to orient yourself to the idiosyncrasies of the market.

Interviews at the AEA Meetings

First-round interviews for the economics job market take place over the three days of the annual AEA meetings and can also take place the day prior to the meeting. These interviews can run anywhere from twenty minutes to an hour.

Calls to schedule these interviews will usually take place in the first two weeks of December. If, by mid-December, you have received few or no calls for AEA interviews, you should contact your advisor immediately so he can contact his colleagues on your behalf. If you leave things too late, people's AEA schedules will have filled up and no amount of importuning from your advisor will help you. If this process seems a bit unfair and non-meritocratic, it is. Although some of these interviews may be perfunctory interviews, held as a courtesy to your advisor, others may have a real prospect of advancing, if, for example, the recruiting department had overlooked your application or thought you would not be interested. Regardless, the more interviews you have, the more you can gain practice in talking about your research. And it never hurts to meet, as part of the coming-out process, people in the profession whom you might encounter later on.

You should not get too down if you do not receive a first-round interview with some of your top choices. Returning to my theme about the randomness of the job market, among the reasons candidates do not receive interview invitations are:

1. They were not looking for someone in your field (this is especially true for apparently open field searches).
2. Even if the ad indicates they are looking for someone in your field, your candidacy or your subfield was not supported by a powerful enough person on the search committee.
3. They already had someone in mind for the position and are running a pro forma search.
4. There are some assistant professors on the market who look better than you because they are safer bets.

5. You were "too good" for them and they didn't think they could attract you.
6. Your advisors trashed you in their letters (kidding—this rarely happens).
7. Your job market paper and vita stank.

Although it is tempting to believe that numbers 6 and 7 are the reasons for not getting interviews, in most cases, it is really a combination of things about the candidate and the needs of the department that result in a candidate's being invited (or not) for an AEA interview. Whether a job candidate secures an interview with a particular department in a specific year really depends on the internal politics of the department at that time and not so much the candidate's qualifications.

With any luck, though, you should have a reasonable number of interviews scheduled for the AEA meetings. During these interviews, you will usually meet with three or four people, one of whom is assigned to be the lead interviewer. She is the one who will have read your file, and will have read or at least skimmed your job market paper. In all likelihood, she will be the only one in the room who knows your field at all, but others who are not familiar with your research area may ask general questions, and you should be prepared to answer questions at any level of detail and sophistication.

The format of the interviews is typically of the following structure. After the introductions and greetings, you will be asked to talk about your job market paper. You start talking about your paper and continue until someone interrupts you to ask a question. You answer the question, and if that does not lead to other follow up questions, you continue with your spiel. More questions will be asked about the paper, often including your research strategy and its validity, your results and whether they should be believed, the paper's significance and where it fits in the literature, what you think of a related or unrelated literature—and you should be prepared to talk about any and all of these aspects of your paper. After this kind of questioning has gone on for some time, the interviewers will ask you about your future research and any papers you have in the works. You should be ready to talk about a coherent research direction on which you plan to embark, and about one specific paper on which you've already done significant work. Despite the heavy emphasis on your job market paper, many an interview has been flubbed because the candidate failed to articulate a specific research agenda or started talking about a paper that they clearly had not done any thinking about or work on.

If you are interviewing in top or upper-middle departments, the interviews can be tough but, depending on the department, can appear disarmingly pleasant. More than likely, your paper will be read carefully and you will be challenged on a number of fronts. The questions asked may be difficult in ways that you may not have anticipated or in ways that can be quite subtle, and it may be hard to gauge whether you have given a sufficiently convincing response. It is generally a good idea to go through your paper with your advisor and any others who know the literature well to identify the ways in which it is vulnerable, and to come up with good responses to potential critiques.

If you are interviewing in mid-ranked or lower-ranked departments, the interview is more of an informational exchange. Much of the tone of the interview is also set by the difference in ranking between your graduating department and the interviewing department. In general, if you come from a much higher-ranked department (or more highly ranked than the typical hire in that department), interviewers will be quite friendly, although you might once in a while encounter someone who is a bit defensive about his work or his own department.

Interviews at liberal arts colleges go somewhat differently. Although you will be asked the usual questions about your job market paper, you will also be asked about teaching, your interests, and more general topics. Interviewers will also care about other ways in which you can contribute to and be a good fit with the college community. If you are interested in jobs at liberal arts colleges, Holmes and Colander 2007 and Owens 2008 provide good background for the specialized recruitment that happens at these places.

At the end of the interview, the interviewers will describe their department and will conclude by asking you whether you have any questions for them. Opinions differ on whether you should ask any questions at this point, but the general rule of thumb is that if the department for which you are interviewing is of the same rank as your own or higher, do not ask any questions; just say that the department's reputation speaks for itself, and that you do not have any questions at this time. If the department is of a much lower rank than your own, you will probably be okay asking a question to show your interest, as long as the question is not particularly critical of the department. And at the very end of the interview, interviewers will usually give you a time frame for when you can expect to hear from them.

The best way to prepare for these interviews is to organize practice interviews with faculty members. Most of the faculty will have gone through multiple iterations of these interviews, either as candidates or as interviewers themselves, so they will know the kinds of things to ask. Many departments will schedule a mock interview or two for their job market candidates, but you will want to schedule more on your own. It is good to have a mix of faculty for the mock interviews—some who are in your research area but who don't know your work, others who are in a completely different research area—to simulate the kinds of questions you will be asked. Those faculty who know your research well will not be as helpful in a mock interview situation (unless they can fake being either hostile or completely ignorant of your work); they can, however, be helpful in pointing out aspects of your research that you should have mentioned but failed to, or in giving specific suggestions on how to better frame your work.

If you are selected for a flyout, you will be contacted during the two or three weeks following the AEA meetings. You may not have much time between the AEA meetings and your first flyout, so be sure to have prepared your job market talk and slides *before* the January meetings.

The average candidate can expect about one flyout for every three AEA interviews, so while the odds are not great, they are not terrible either. Again, you should not get discouraged if you do not receive a flyout invitation from some of the places that interviewed you. There can be any number of mysterious reasons for your candidacy's not progressing, and it can be very difficult to gauge on the basis of the first-round interview ("but they were so nice to me!") whether you will get a flyout. It is frequently the case that candidates are interviewed because their work looks interesting or a faculty member wants to meet them, and not because they are really a serious candidate for the position. Consider this kind of interview good practice and an opportunity to meet people who may be interested in you later on.

Flyouts

If all goes well, you will be invited for flyouts or campus visits. These visits usually take one to two days and are pretty standardized. You will be expected to give a job talk, about the length of a typical seminar (an hour and a half to two hours), on your job market paper. You will have one-on-one meetings (each usually half an hour to an hour) with various members of the faculty, including the chair of the department and the search committee chair. There is also typically a meeting with the dean, who will go over institutional details and the formal tenure process; depending on the interests of the dean, he may also want to talk about your research. Occasionally, you will meet with graduate students. There will likely be breakfast meetings, lunch meetings, and a dinner or two at some fancy restaurant.

Be prepared for long days during your flyouts. Particularly if it's a big department, breakfast meetings start early, and when you are not giving your job talk, you will be in meetings all day. You may have a short break between your last meeting and dinner, but don't plan on it, and so the typical day will end around 9:00 P.M.

Expenses incurred during the flyout, such as travel and hotel accommodations, are paid by the department flying you out. You may occasionally have to pay your expenses up front, especially if you book your own flight, but the department will reimburse you (although this may take a couple of months).

One thing to remember is that, by the time you reach the flyout stage, at least a few people are already interested in your research, and any candidate that a department flies out will be a reasonable choice. The purpose of the flyout, then, is really to assess how well you would fit into the department and how likable a colleague you are. By likable, I don't mean life-of-the-party likable—we're talking about economists here—but more of, would-be-an-interesting-and-collegial-person likable.

Although one-on-one faculty meetings are important for this assessment, the job talk is perhaps even more important, since not everyone who is part of the decision-making process will be able to schedule a meeting with you. For this reason, a terrific job market presentation can put you over the top. Very few people will have read your job market paper, so they will rely on your job talk to get a sense of you and your research.

In preparing for your talk, there are three important things to keep in mind. First, the job talk has to be understandable to everyone in the department, especially those who are not specialists in your area. Thus, it is imperative that you motivate your research (in the presentation) so that any Joe Economist will agree that your research is important. In addition, you should take care not to burden your slides with detail and jargon that only those working in your area will understand. When in doubt as to whether something is too technical, dumb it down. Those working in your field will be sure to ask the right technical questions, and you should be prepared to answer those, but avoid putting those things in your main presentation.

Second, your talk should be polished. You should not be putting together slides at the last minute, and you should not be changing your slides at the last minute.[2] You should know every slide you will use, the order in which you will use them, and exactly what you wish to say at every slide. This means you should practice, practice, and practice, and then practice some more. But don't memorize your presentation; your talk should sound polished but not over-rehearsed.

Finally, many students focus on preparing their slides, but neglect to consider that an important part of the job talk is being able to handle questions well. More than a few job candidates in the history of mankind have lost potential job offers because they responded poorly to questions that were asked. The main way that candidates mess up the Q&A is by responding hostilely or dismissively to questions. Even though your first instinct may be to be aggressive, especially in response to a question that you perceive as critical or stupid, it is crucial that you set aside that first reaction and respond non-defensively. Answer all questions respectfully and try to address the questioners' concerns. Never get into an argument with the questioner. Even if you are absolutely correct, make your assertion, concede that there may be alternative viewpoints, and note that you will have to think about the questioner's point some more. Say all this in the most polite tone that you can muster. Since this is a job talk, not a political debate, it's almost always better to look a bit weak than to look like a major-league jerk (although of course, try to avoid looking like either).

Getting the tone right is important for the rest of the flyout as well. Although each department has its own culture—some more serious, others more relaxed—most are looking for a polite, interesting person who is intellectually engaged. You should be yourself, of course, since having all parties be honest about who they are results in an optimal match. But don't loosen up so much that you end up acting like a clueless boor; this is still an interview. Perhaps the best way to think about flyouts is that you should try to be the best possible version of yourself.

Offers and Negotiations

An offer is usually made to the department's top choice candidate shortly after all flyouts have been completed. As in the earlier stages, the choice of a final candidate is a mysterious and unpredictable process. Sometimes, it truly is about who gave the most polished presentation and came off best during meetings. Other times, there may be much *Sturm und Drang* within the department, with one faction favoring one candidate and another supporting a second candidate; if these two factions cannot amicably resolve their differences, the

offer may go to a third compromise candidate who is not enthusi-
astically supported by either camp. These things are hard to divine.
For every department that votes against you for apparently arbitrary
reasons, another will equally arbitrarily vote for you. The only thing
you can do is to be the best version of yourself during your flyouts
and (after sending your thank-you e-mails) trust that the numbers
work in your favor.

If an offer is forthcoming, you will typically receive an e-mail or a
phone call with a few details of the offer. You will want (in fact, need)
to receive a written letter detailing specifics of the offer. These specifics include salary, research start-up funds, other (e.g., travel) funds,
research assistants, administrative support, leaves of absence, and
reimbursement for moving expenses. Remember that the chair can
promise whatever she wants on the phone, but unless and until you
receive the offer in writing, *there is no offer*. (People differ on how
much a chair's verbal offer can be trusted and do not view the verbal
offer as simply cheap talk. My view is that it would be very costly for
you to enforce the terms of a verbal offer if the chair doesn't stick to
some of the initial terms, and since my interest is in making sure that
you as a candidate don't get taken advantage of, I take the conservative view of counseling you to keep all your options open until you
have an offer in writing.)

You will be expected to negotiate the terms of the initial offer. Of
course, if you hate this kind of thing, you can accept the initial offer
right away, but you would probably be leaving money on the table.
In principle, all of the things I mentioned are negotiable, by which
I mean, you can and should start by asking for more of all of them,
although the department is unlikely to grant all of your requests. The
department will respond with a counteroffer, and you can work from
there, holding firm on the things that you value most and dropping
demands for the things that you value least. By the way, now is the
time to mention your spouse and to ask what the department can do
to help him find a job at your new location. If you ask, the department will usually pay for you and your family to visit the campus for
a second look before you decide on the offer.

If you receive multiple offers, you could in principle negotiate with all of the parties and pit one against the other to get the best package that you can. It would be considered bad form and terribly tacky, but you could certainly do this. Alternatively, what most chairs prefer, and what is most polite, is to decide which department is your top choice, decide what it would take for you to accept an offer there, and negotiate with them first. If they appear unable or unwilling to accommodate your demands, begin negotiating with your second-choice school; sometimes, your first choice department may be able to see the light and find some way to meet your demands if they see that a peer institution is able to offer the package you want.

You should not accept an offer until you have received all the offers that you are going to get. That way, you can make an informed decision based on all the options available to you. Some candidates find that they are faced with an offer to which they have to respond within a very short time frame, before they are able to finish their campus visits, or before other potential employers have reached a decision. It is reasonable to request an extension so that you are able to make an informed choice (and you should definitely do this), but some employers may not particularly care whether you make a fully informed decision, as they are playing their own pernicious games with other employers and other candidates. More charitably, employers may be under their own time constraints or have other good backup candidates that they would not like to lose in the event that you decline. Given this possibility, to the extent that you have some discretion in your travels, you should try to organize trips to your top choices early among your campus visits. The one caveat to this advice is that there is a lot of learning-by-doing that happens on campus visits so you are bound to make a lot of mistakes during your first flyout, with presumably fewer mistakes during subsequent flyouts. Try to have your first campus visit be at a less preferred (for you) place so that you can make your mistakes early in a lower-stakes environment.

Related to the issue of timing, after you accept an offer, it may happen that you receive a better offer, and you may be tempted to renege on the accepted offer. This is a terrible idea. You work in an extremely small profession, and if you renege, the damage in terms of your long-term reputation will be much greater than any short-term benefit you get from backing out of your acceptance. Realize that because you accepted the earlier offer, that department would have already called an end to its search and may have lost the opportunity to hire this year. If you renege, they will be unable to hire anyone else, and they won't be happy about it. Plus, if the other department wanted to hire you this year, they will likely be interested in you later on when you may have more mobility. So, once you have accepted an offer, follow through with it. Being able to trust one's colleagues—their work and their word—is paramount in this profession, so don't mess up your future by doing anything that damages that trust.

Bad Market Outcomes

What should you do if, God forbid, you don't receive any offers or don't receive any offers you like? The problem of not receiving any offers is in some ways the easier problem. If you don't receive any offers, then your only options are to be unemployed or to stay in grad school for one more year. In most cases, staying in grad school dominates being unemployed. During this additional year, though, you don't want to do more of the same things you did last year. You want to review your job market experience, identify where you could have done better, work on improving your job market paper or coming up with a better one, and in general, put your time to good use.

What if your problem is not that you didn't receive any offers, but that you didn't receive any offers that you like? Suppose you had your heart set on an academic job and you only received private sector offers. Or you received offers from low-ranking departments but think you can do better. Should you turn down the offers you received and stay in grad school an extra year, or should you accept what you've got and move on from there?

Your optimal choice depends on your level of risk-aversion and your ability to identify where things went wrong for you with the job market. You should engage in careful reflection and talk to your advisors to brutally dissect your job market experience and identify concrete ways in which your application could have been improved. What was it about your job market paper? Could you have improved on your job market talk? Were there things that you did or said during campus visits that sabotaged your chances?

But be careful, there are always things someone could have done to be a better candidate. For example, all of us, given an extra year, would be able to write a better job market paper. But the crucial issue is, how much better would the paper be? And how much would these changes improve your chances on the market? If the job market topic is simply uninteresting or unimportant, refining a proof is unlikely to help you. Adding a new data set may add something to the paper, but it will not improve your odds very much. You can always do more, but what's the realistic size of the expected payoff?

If after reflection, it looks as though the changes you would be able to make in one year would not result in a huge increase in payoff, or if the consensus among your advisors is that "there is a lot of randomness in the market," you should accept one of the offers you've received and move on from there. From that position, you can then strategize how to go where you want to go next.

I am of the opinion that it is almost always better to be in a serious paying job than to be in grad school if you are about to finish your Ph.D. You will have more job security, you will almost surely have a higher income, and you will gain experience being a professional economist that will undoubtedly help you in your future research and your second attempt at the job market. As long as you are still doing something in the field of economics or a closely related area, you should be able to plan for a transition to a more preferred job. It won't be easy and will require using your free time to prepare, but you can make it happen.

One successful strategy to insure against a bad outcome is to apply for postdoctoral fellowships at the same time you are on the market. I discussed postdoctoral fellowships in some detail in an earlier section of this chapter ("When to Go on the Job Market"), so you should refer back to that if you are considering this option.

Although the application process for postdocs (except for the top ones I mentioned) is not as time-consuming as for tenure-track jobs—for example, most of them do not require interviews or job talks—one downside is that there is no central clearinghouse for economics postdoctoral fellowships (many are not advertised on JOE). This means that you will have to do a bit of work even to find out about the fellowships and then complete a separate application for each one. You should also know that some postdoc deadlines can be much earlier than the typical economics tenure-track deadlines, although some—especially those looking to scoop up unlucky students from the regular market—can be as late as March or April.

Most postdocs are institutionally funded and their availability varies from year to year. Your best bet is to talk to faculty at your home institution and faculty at institutions where you are interested in doing a postdoc to see if they know of any fellowships. You can also do some research online or at your graduate fellowships office to look for social science postdocs.

If you receive both a good tenure-track offer and a good postdoc, many departments will allow you to defer the tenure-track position to pursue the postdoc. I would say that overall postdocs are a good hedge for the job market, and a good postdoc—one that gives you free time to pursue your own research—can be a very productive way to spend the first several years of your post-Ph.D. life.

Looking Ahead

Coming into the job market process, most students believe that they will place in a department that is of the same or slightly lesser rank than their home institution. According to Stock, Alston, and Milkman (2000), however, the average Ph.D. graduate is placed at an institution that is about sixty (that's right, 60) rank positions below the institution at which they received their degree. This means that you will most likely be working in a department that does not have all of the physical, financial, and human capital that you are used to. Students are frequently disappointed with this outcome.

But this feeling is fleeting. Your new job presents a great opportunity. You will be able to pursue whatever research you like and to develop your leadership and mentoring skills. Instead of always looking up to Big Powerful Professor, you will have students looking at you to guide them. Your new colleagues will expect you to contribute as an equal, to get the job done, to take on leadership roles. And you may find that you like these new responsibilities and are good at them. You will learn to take your place at the table as a peer, and you will have earned it.

Notes

1. In fact, most top and near-top departments never read unsolicited applications. These departments rely on word-of-mouth to draw up their list of possible candidates, having been informed about top students by faculty in other departments. So the applications that you send these places, if you haven't been asked to submit an application, will go in the electronic recycle bin unread.

2. If you think of an additional analysis while you're on the road, you should still create that slide, but include it with your supplementary slides at the end. In your talk, you can refer to that analysis but leave the detailed discussion to the Q&A period at the end.

References

Coles, Peter, John Cawley, Phillip B. Levine, Muriel Niederle, Alvin E. Roth, and John J. Seigfried. 2010. "The Job Market for New Economists: A Market Design Perspective." *Journal of Economic Perspectives* 24: 187–206.

Holmes, Jessica, and David Colander. 2007. "The Hiring of an Economist: A Case Study." *American Economist* 51: 54–62.

Owens, Mark F. 2008. "The Search for an Economics Job with a Teaching Focus." *Journal for Economic Educators* 8: 7–27.

Stock, Wendy A., Richard M. Alston, and Martin Milkman. 2000. "The Academic Labor Market for Economists: 1995–96." *Atlantic Economics Journal* 28: 164–185.

Further Reading

Cawley, John. 2011. "A Guide (and Advice) for Economists on the U.S. Junior Academic Job Market." *Job Openings for Economists.*
Siegfried, John J., and Wendy A. Stock. 1999. "The Labor Market for New Ph.D. Economists." *Journal of Economic Perspectives* 13: 115–134.
Siegfried, John J. and Wendy A. Stock. 2004. "The Market for New Ph.D. Economists in 2002." *American Economic Review Papers and Proceedings* 94: 272–285.

Useful Web Pages

Advice from Famous Economists

- David Levine: http://faculty.haas.berkeley.edu/levine/cheap_advice.html

Job Openings for Economists

- http://www.aeaweb.org/joe/

Economics Job Market Wiki

- www.econjobrumors.com/wiki.php

Econjobmarket.org

- https://econjobmarket.org/

Economics Job Market Rumors (use at your own risk—lots of misinformation, trolling, potentially offensive commentary)

- http://www.econjobrumors.com/

Chapter 9

Conclusion: The Ph.D. Economist-at-Large

According to the Bureau of Labor Statistics, there are fewer than sixteen thousand economists working in the United States.[1] It's a small club. If someone gathered all of us in a football stadium in a medium-sized American city, we wouldn't even fill three-fourths of the stadium.

And yet economists wield enormous influence in American society. We are in charge of the Federal Reserve and the Treasury and, through various advisory councils, we have the ear of the President and Congress. Wall Street also pays attention to us, as do universities and think tanks. And we influence the public and the general discourse through newspaper columns, op-ed pieces, blogs, and talking head appearances.

At least part of the reason for this broad scope of influence is that economics is a powerful tool for analyzing many important phenomena in the world. More relevant for you, getting a Ph.D. in economics is excellent training in using this valuable tool. As you have seen by now, obtaining a Ph.D. in economics is not painless but it is far from impossible. A reasonable if aggressively simplified take-away from this book is that successfully getting a Ph.D. in economics—being trained in the profession of economic research, as I argued in Chapter 1—means that you simply need to:

- prepare yourself with the appropriate analytical, mathematical, and research tools before you enter graduate school;
- take your graduate school application seriously;
- apply yourself diligently to your courses and exams;
- put in the hours and effort to develop multiple ideas for your dissertation;
- develop the intellectual and social-psychological discipline required to be a professional in this field;
- put it all together in a polished package to take to the job market.

This is all quite doable but requires a commitment on the scale of years. The intellectual and professional rewards, however, are immense. If you work as an academic economist, you get great intellectual freedom: you can read, learn about, analyze, and work on whatever topic interests you. You work with and get challenged by smart people with interesting ideas. You get paid well compared to many others in academia and sufficiently well to have a comfortable life. You have useful analytical and quantitative skills that are valuable outside of academia, so you can work as a consultant in the nonprofit or private sector on real-world projects. You have an opportunity to influence the economic understanding of young students who will then go on to contribute thoughtfully to society. And you have a level of flexibility in your time that is rarely found in other occupations.

If you become a professional economist outside of the academy, you have many of these attractive benefits as well. Although you may have somewhat less flexibility on your projects, you will be able to work on intellectually challenging real-world projects. In this applied world, you will have the opportunity to make a measurable difference in the lives of others. Although you may have less flexibility in your work hours, the time demands tend to be more limited and better defined than in academia, and your time outside of the office is your own. And you will certainly be remunerated very well. There is much to like about being a Ph.D. economist, regardless of which track you choose.

The Afterlife and the Economist-at-Large

A fear that many graduates have is that they will be trapped into working on their dissertation topic for the rest of their lives. This thought fills them with dread, because by the time they've worked several years on their dissertation and presented their job market paper half a bijillion times, they will be utterly sick of it and never want to see it or speak of it again. And this is even before the paper goes through the publication mill, being submitted, reviewed, rejected, revised, and resubmitted. So any nausea associated with your dissertation is understandable.

Bear in mind that there is nothing in your contract that stipulates that you must work on your dissertation topic in subsequent work although it is always sensible to build on your previous knowledge. But perhaps your previous research efforts showed you how foolhardy or difficult your dissertation topic was. In that case, you would be wise to move on. And if you carefully read the CVs of mid-career professors, you will see that many of these faculty are writing on quite different topics from what they wrote on when they were just out of graduate school. Anecdotally, most scholars go through ten-year cycles in their work; that is, they work intensively on a topic for ten years, then switch to a new topic for the next ten years, and so on. This is a natural progression, so you don't need to worry that you will be trapped working on any given research topic.

If you become an academic economist, you should focus on your trade first. By this I mean that you should focus on becoming a good researcher and a good teacher. Develop the technical skills required to be a good researcher in your topic of interest and the communication skills required to be a good teacher. This should be your first priority. But also give a little bit of thought to how you would like to be an economist in the world. Economics is not simply about abstractions, although there is a good deal of abstraction in economics. An important part of economics is explaining why certain things happen (or don't happen) in the real world. We use mathematics to do so, but economics is different from pure mathematics; it is rooted in concrete events and social phenomena. For this reason, economists are well suited to be engaged in the world and to make a contribution to public discourse on economic matters (broadly defined).

While engagement in the world is by no means required—you may choose to spend all your time on purely academic matters—I urge that you think about the ways that you might be an economist-at-large in the world. This might be through traditional means, such as acting as a consultant or policy advisor, but it could also be through op-eds, blogging, or media appearances. It could be something as simple as giving a talk to a local business group, giving *pro bono* advice to a charitable organization, or delivering a guest lecture to middle school or high school students. Your training has given you a useful way of analyzing problems and interpreting events, and your insights may be helpful to others.

And while economics is very powerful in explaining many things, a second farewell exhortation that I have for you is also to realize the limits of economics. Today's economics is not the same as it was in the days of Adam Smith, nor in the heyday of 1950s Keynesianism, nor in the go-go times of the 1980s neoclassical resurgence. Economists and the economics literature move on. We make mistakes with our models, we learn, we make better models. While it is tempting to view the canonical economics that you learned in graduate school as The Way the World Works, you should realize that our current models may be incomplete or misleading. You, I hope, will be building on this literature to move us to a better literature, and we should talk amongst ourselves about how to do this. But we should also talk to non-economists. To remain knowledgeable and relevant, we should be engaging with the ideas of those outside our discipline—psychologists, sociologists, political scientists, biological and physical scientists, artists and writers, business people, Uncle Frank and Aunt Nellie—and thinking about how to incorporate some of their insights into our work. Of course, not all ideas will be equally useful, but we should be open to developments from quarters other than economics. To thrive as a discipline that makes real contributions, economics must be continually developing, and economists should be learning from others.

Finally, since economists do not know everything—and since this economist in particular does not know everything—if you have helpful suggestions, information, or resources that you think have been overlooked in this book, please feel free to contact me through the University of Pennsylvania Press.

Graduate school in economics can be tough. And it can be rewarding. And I hope you will find that it is only the beginning of a very gratifying career, which few of us would trade for anything else.

Notes

1. This number consists primarily of individuals who have Ph.D. degrees, but can include people with master's or bachelor's degrees who work in jobs identified by the Standard Occupational Classification code of 19-3011.

Index

admissions/applying to economics programs, 14–35; and department politics, 15–16; and department rankings, 17, 20, 23, 24, 27–31; grades/coursework (undergraduate), 17, 19–22; GRE, 14, 17–19; and international students, 46, 106; personal statement, 14, 26–27; recommendation letters, 14, 22–24, 33–34; research experience, 23–25, 32; social influences, 35. *See also* undergraduate preparation

advisors/dissertation committee, 68–69; and employment opportunities, 118, 120; and job market timing, 115–16; oral exam, 69, 81–83; selection, 63, 78–81

Alston, Richard M., 134

ambition, 25

American Economic Association, 11, 69, 104, 117, 123–27

Amir, Rabah, 29

applying to economics programs. *See* admissions/applying to economics programs

attrition rates, 93

bad reasons to enter economics Ph.D. programs, 4–6

Basalla, Susan, 95

Bellman techniques, 43

blogging, 20, 34, 137

careers of Ph.D. economists, 3–4, 80–81, 137–41

Colander, David, 125

Coles, Peter, 122

Columbia University, 13 n.5

commitment, graduate school as, 8, 138

committee. *See* advisors/dissertation committee

competition, 39, 59, 89

completion rates, 93

consumer theory, 41

core content of economics, 44–45

Council of Economic Advisors, 32

coursework. *See under* first-year courses; second year; undergraduate preparation

curriculum vitae, 117–18

Debelius, Maggie, 95

Diploma programs in economics, 12 n.4

discriminatory behavior, 97–98, 99–100, 103, 105, 111

dissertations, 68–69, 78, 82–83, 91, 139. *See also* advisors/dissertation committee; research, independent

diversity, 15–16

econjobmarket.org, 118

econometrics, 19, 38, 41, 43

emotional health. *See* mental/emotional health

employment search/opportunities, 69, 114–35; "scramble," 122; careers of Ph.D. economists, 3–4, 80–81, 137–41; and department ranking, 28–29, 31, 35–36 n.1, 118–19, 134,

employment search *(cont.)*
135 n.1; failing to find a job, 132–34;
flyouts, 119–20, 126–29, 131, 133;
and grades, 56; and international
students, 111–13; interviews (AEA
meeting), 119, 121, 123–27; when to
start looking, 115–17. *See also* job
market paper; job market talk
enrollment rates, 11, 12–13 n.5
European master's programs, 9, 10
exams: first year, 53–54, 57–58; oral, 69,
81–83; second year, 66
experimental economics, 117
extracurricular activities, 54–56, 67

faculty members: and admission
criteria, 15–16, 21, 27; admissions
influence, 28–29, 30; and choosing
a department, 31; and employment
opportunities, 118–19, 126; and first-
year students, 59; and gender, 98,
99, 101, 103–4; international student
relationships, 105, 109–10, 112; and
job market process, 118–19; romantic
relationships with, 90–91; and
second-year students, 65; and sexual
harassment, 101–3; student reputations with, 56; teaching assistant
expectations of, 108–9; and working
groups, 74. *See also* advisors/disserta-
tion committee
Federal Reserve Banks, 23, 32
fellowships, 15
finance programs, 12 n.3
financial aid, 15, 29–30, 55, 85–86
first year, 38–60; breadth of, 44–45, 62;
difficulties, 38–40, 55–56, 59–60;
exam preparation, 53–54, 57–58; importance of mathematics preparation
for, 19–20, 42–44, 46–47; structure/
substance, 41–44; study strategies,
48–54; succeeding in, 45–48, 56;
weeding-out process, 40, 57, 58–59
flyouts, 119–20, 126–29, 131, 133

game theory, 19, 41
gender. *See* women in economics
programs

general equilibrium theory, 41
good reasons to enter economics Ph.D.
programs, 6–7
grades/coursework (undergraduate),
17, 19–22, 105–6
GRE (Graduate Record Examinations),
14, 17–19
Grijalva, Therese C., 27

Hamiltonian techniques, 43
Hansen, W. Lee, 12–13 n.5
Harvard Society of Fellows, 116
Harvard University, 12–13 n.5, 29
Holmes, Jessica, 125

ideas, research, 70, 72
independence, 70, 71–72
independent research. *See* research,
independent
international students, 97–98, 104–13;
and employment, 111–13; faculty
relationships, 105, 109–10, 112; language difficulties, 104–5, 106–8, 111;
percentage of degrees awarded, 11;
social support, 105, 110–11; teaching
difficulties, 105, 107–9; technical
preparation, 45–46, 105–6
intuition, 12 n.4, 42

job market paper: finding ideas for,
75–76; and group projects, 77;
importance of, 115; improving, 125,
132–33; and literature, 124, 125;
submitting, 117–18; when to finish,
116. *See also* employment search/
opportunities
job market talk: at AEA interviews, 124–
25; at flyouts, 127, 128–29; improving,
133; relationship with paper, 116;
as teaching preparation, 86. *See also*
employment search/opportunities
Job Openings for Economists (JOE),
117, 134
job search. *See* employment search/
opportunities

Kalaitzidakis, Pantelis, 27
Knauff, Malgorzata, 29